THE AGE OF THE BATTLESHIP

⚓

THE WATTS HISTORIES OF
THE UNITED STATES NAVY

⚓

THE AGE OF
THE BATTLESHIP
1890-1922

⚓

By Brayton Harris

LIEUTENANT COMMANDER, U.S.N.R.

FRANKLIN WATTS, INC.
575 Lexington Avenue, New York, N.Y. 10022

Contents
⚓

This book is respectfully dedicated to that small—incredibly small—band of naval officers who somehow managed, with all the odds against them, to bring our Navy from a position of pitiable inconsequence to a position of unchallenged preeminence.

And is lovingly dedicated to my wife Nancy, who somehow managed to survive the sometimes hectic hours connected with the production of this book, while at the same time producing a more notable work of her own, our son Kirkpatrick.

ONE

⚓

The New Navy

*The world holds still for no nation, and
only the blind could not see that there
were big changes ahead.*

—THEODORE ROOSEVELT

IT WAS the end of an era; and a beginning.

The mighty westward movement of American pioneers had led to
the settlement of the plains and mountains; the last battle of the
Indian Wars which had lasted through almost three centuries was
soon to be fought; and 200,000 miles of railroad track were lacing
the country. The farmer and the businessman were now replacing
the pioneer; the pioneer, ill at ease amidst such progress, began
looking for the next frontier.

The United States of America was the fastest growing country in
the world. The population was to double in the thirty years following the Civil War, and by 1880, with the enfeebling debts of that
war almost eliminated, the United States had money to match its
energy. It had fathered a growing industrial giant that would soon
dominate the commerce of the world; and as the nation grew in
wealth, the growing markets of the West were no longer sufficient to
absorb the total output of the growing industries of the East. The
community of merchants began to seek new outlets abroad.

The antimilitary prejudices of the immediate postwar period,
when the nation was both sickened and impoverished by war, had

died out. By 1880 the nation could once again acknowledge the existence of and the need for a standing army and navy. And it could also expect the comfort and protection that the military could offer, especially in the remote overseas areas where trade was being developed but where, perhaps, respect for the American flag had not yet arrived. It was, primarily, to the Navy that this expectation was directed. To the Navy, whose peacetime duties included "protection and advancement of American commerce . . . protection of American life and property endangered by wars between foreign countries . . . and service in support of American policy in matters where foreign countries are concerned." To the Navy, which, through indifference, indecision, and political corruption, had almost ceased to exist, and which probably could have been beaten in a fair fight by any of the modern warships that several South American neighbors were then acquiring.

Increasing public interest in the Navy finally prompted that service to take stock of itself; and the stock was small indeed. In November 1881, alarmed and anxious for the future, Secretary of the Navy William H. Hunt petitioned President Chester A. Arthur as follows:

> SIR: The condition of the Navy imperatively demands the prompt and earnest attention of Congress . . . [or] . . . it must soon dwindle into insignificance.

Secretary Hunt hesitated to admit that the Navy was already insignificant; yet that fact was painfully evident. From a Civil War peak of 700 ships—among them some of the most advanced designs in any navy in the world—the U.S. Navy had fallen to a point where, in 1881, it consisted of only 26 more or less effective ships. Of these, only 4 of the smallest were so modern as to have iron hulls. The United States claimed to have a fleet of 20 armored ships, but any observer wishing to verify this claim would have found himself making a tour of shipyards in order to count the unfinished ships of outmoded design that had been "under construction" since the Civil

War. Indeed, not one of these armored ships was in service in 1881. By comparison, the British navy had almost 400 active ships in use that year, 56 of which were armored. Even the newly awakened nation of Japan, which had not started a navy until it purchased a ship from the United States in 1866, could boast a fleet of 19 ships, 5 of which were armored and most of which were relatively new.

The guiding policy under which the U.S. Navy was being maintained—if there was any policy at all—was believed to be in keeping with the wishes of the men who had framed the Constitution. As Congressman (later President) James A. Garfield reiterated in an 1878 speech in the House of Representatives: "Our fathers said: 'Though we will use the taxing power to maintain a small Army and Navy sufficient to keep alive the knowledge of war, yet the main reliance for our defense shall be the intelligence, culture, and skill of our people.' "

This was a nice sentiment, but it ignored one basic fact: the weapons of war, especially naval war, were changing rapidly, and the United States was making no effort to keep abreast of those changes. Perhaps "ignored" is not the proper term; "side-stepped" is more accurate. Members of Congress—who controlled the funds—acknowledged the changes, but branded them as "costly experimentation" being carried on by the navies of Europe. These experiments included many advances which had been invented by, introduced by, or combat-tested by the U.S. Navy—armor on ships; steamships without the encumbrance of sails; guns with rifled barrels; guns mounted in revolving turrets. The U.S. Navy had been the first in the world to build a steamship; the first to build a steamship using a submerged screw propeller; and, just after the Civil War, it had built the fastest ship in the world. This was the USS *Wampanoag*, which under steam achieved the then remarkable speed of 17.75 knots, while the best of the famed clipper ships rarely exceeded 15 knots.

But in the years following the Civil War, the Navy and Congress effectively rejected all this progress. Full sail rigs were ordered on

[3]

the steamships; efficient screw propellers were replaced with low-drag models that were practically useless under steam but would minimize interference with ships under sail; the fastest ship in the world had its boiler power reduced "for reasons of economy." These moves were all taken in the name of "economy." Navy regulations of 1870 expressly forbade the use of steam power, except when a commanding officer was convinced that such use was absolutely necessary. Commanding officers were cautioned that if the Navy Department did not agree with the justification in any given instance, they themselves might be called upon to pay for any coal that had been used!

Economy in operations was, as always, a desirable thing. However, these retrogressions were not so much motivated by a wish to save money as they were a reaction by a group of senior naval officers who harbored a solid and lasting dislike for steam. Steam, somehow, just was not proper. It was dirty. It was the work of greasy-handed engineers, not true naval officers.

And, while these officers were busy economizing, the rest of the Navy managed to spend over fifty million dollars in ostensibly maintaining ships and equipment. But, what with a little graft here, a little favoritism there, and much political maneuvering everywhere, there never seemed to be anything to show for the money. Most of it was spent on the periodic overhaul of ships that were worthless and should have been replaced. In fact, there were rumors that the only reason the Navy kept some of these ships in service was that they provided continuing employment for workers in both naval and civilian shipyards. Politically, shipyards were very strong.

Even some reasonably useful ships spent most of their lives in the shipyards. The *Tennessee,* built in 1869, was in active service only three months during the six years following her commissioning. The rest of the time she was being repaired and overhauled at a cost greater than her replacement value. Suspicion of corruption in the handling of this matter and others was strong, but it was often hard to tell just who might be responsible. The organization of the

[4]

Navy Department was so loose that work was frequently undertaken without authorization, or even any real determination of need. For example, a proposal to repair a ship—or let a contract, or buy supplies—would filter through the various bureaus, each of which jealously guarded its independence and avoided either coordination or cooperation with any of the others. The proposal would eventually reach the desk of the Secretary, who would add his signature to all of the others. And no one would have actually studied the proposal. Such a system was made-to-order for graft, and it is no surprise that graft occurred. Nor is it any surprise that much of the work undertaken was actually worthless.

About the year 1880, for example, someone decided that it was time to rebuild the *Omaha*. The fact that this ship was a completely obsolete wooden vessel and not worth keeping in the fleet made little difference. A half million dollars was spent on her overhaul, which was more than it would have cost to build a new and modern ship of a comparable type. In rebuilding her, the various bureaus had been so concerned with their own interests and had appropriated whatever space on board could be used for their own programs that when the *Omaha* once again put to sea in 1884 it was discovered that they had left room for enough coal for only four days' steaming.

True, there were scandals and congressional investigations, but they always seemed to be intended more to embarrass the rival political party than to bring about any real reforms. The system did not change; only the names of the men who ran it. Moreover, there was nothing to guarantee that, even if they were honest, they had enough intelligence or experience to recognize malfeasance when they saw it. The post of Secretary of the Navy, which carried with it as much power as the incumbent chose to exercise, was normally filled on a strictly political basis. Appointees were selected to appease business interests in the East, or agrarian interests in the South, or to pay a debt to a faithful supporter. Indeed, it was only by accident that the position was ever filled by a man who even had an interest in the Navy. While the story may be apocryphal, it is reported that the Secretary of the Navy under President Rutherford B. Hayes (1877–81) was so ignorant of naval matters that he was surprised, upon assuming office, to discover that ships were hollow!

Fortunately for the Navy (and the nation) a series of beneficial accidents eventually filled the position with interested and dedicated men. William H. Hunt, as already noted, insisted on bringing the true condition of the fleet to the attention of Congress and the public; his predecessors simply had been content to issue innocuous and inaccurate yearly reports. Following President Garfield's assassination, Hunt resigned and was succeeded by William E. Chandler, who carried on the crusade. Chandler has been criticized—and justly so—for a number of indiscretions in office, not the least of which was the awarding of shipbuilding contracts to a good friend of his who, as a shipbuilder, was incompetent. Be that as it may, however, Chandler pushed for a better Navy. He induced Congress to pass legislation prohibiting repairs to old wooden ships if the cost of such repairs would exceed 30 per cent (later reduced to 20 per cent) of the cost of building a new replacement. He further prodded Congress to direct action by suggesting that if the Navy were not brought up to date it should be disbanded and its annual expenditures "be reserved to procure, in national emergencies, the assistance of foreign ships and guns." Of course, such a procedure would have been an insult to a nation whose most publicized trait was self-reliance. Accordingly, Congress accepted the challenge and within six months had authorized construction of four new ships—the first of any type in over ten years.

Naval historians often refer to this congressional authorization as marking "the rise of the new Navy." If in reality it was more of a bump on the historical landscape than a rise, it was at least an honest start. The act of March 3, 1883, resulted in the addition of the cruisers *Atlanta, Boston,* and *Chicago,* and the dispatch boat *Dolphin.* Known, because of the convenient order of their names, as the ABCD fleet, they were the first test of American designers' and

[6]

shipbuilders' skill in constructing modern warships. The fact that they were for the most part failures does not detract from the importance of the effort.

In comparison with contemporary European designs, the ABCD ships were sadly deficient. Intended to be "fully modern," they were the first ships of the U.S. Navy to have steel hulls; and yet, each carried a full sail rig. The *Dolphin* was later officially characterized as "more of a pleasure boat than a warship." The cruisers did not meet the expectations of their designers; construction was intermittently delayed because of faulty specifications and changes in the plans; and the contractor—the good friend of Secretary Chandler—was unable to complete the ships. Under orders from William C. Whitney, Chandler's successor, the government took control of the unfinished ships and, in the contractor's yard, using his workmen, supervised the final stages of construction.

In 1885, authorizations were obtained for four more ships—two cruisers and two gunboats. The Navy Department, recognizing that mistakes had been made in the designs of the ABCD ships, based these later ships on the best of European designs. Additionally, since two of the ABCD's were completed before the contracts for the new ships were drawn up, the Navy was able to take advantage of one lesson. The *Dolphin* and the *Atlanta* had failed to meet performance specifications on their official acceptance trials. It would be difficult to determine if this was solely the fault of the contractor or whether the government had to share the responsibility; however, for a number of years, subsequent shipbuilding contracts included a clause imposing penalties on the builder for failure to meet specifications of speed or horsepower, and at the same time provided for a bonus if the specifications were exceeded.

These authorizations of 1883 and 1885 started the Navy well and truly on the way toward rebirth. But cruisers alone do not make up a fleet, and the major problem facing the Navy throughout the rest of the nineteenth century was the determination of what types of ships, and in what proportion, should be designed and built. A corollary problem was to convince Congress of the validity of any proposed program.

In the long run, it is considerations of strategy that must in large part determine the physical composition of a fleet. Until 1890, the dominant naval strategy of the United States, unchanged for a hundred years despite the problems it caused in various wars along the way, envisioned a two-part operation, each to be handled by a specific type of ship. The first part was "coast defense"—a fleet of small but powerful armored ships designed specifically to operate within harbors and shallow coastal waters and nowhere else. The other part was "commerce raiding," to be accomplished by swift, lightly armed cruisers that could overtake and capture enemy merchantmen but could also run away from a serious fight if necessary. A few miscellaneous types of ships would be required for logistic support or carrying dispatches, but these were considered to be of minimal importance. The one single most useful type of ship for both wartime and peacetime service was the unarmored cruiser. Cheap to build, inexpensive to maintain, and mechanically unsophisticated, it was the natural focus of the American warship-building effort through the 1880's.

But the exploding technology of the period forced a multiplication of ship types and subtypes, and even within the framework of the accepted strategy, choices had to be made. The fighting ships of an earlier day had been distinguished from each other primarily by their size—and, in direct proportion, by the number of guns they could therefore carry. Specialization per se was minimal; but as ships became more and more complicated and expensive, specialization became imperative. In any instance, design had to be a compromise between such factors as speed, endurance, fuel capacity, armor, armament, and cost. Size was no longer a distinguishing or determining factor.

Speed and armor protection, other things being equal, were inversely proportionate. The thicker the armor, the better able the

[8]

ship was to withstand heavy gunfire but the more limited it was in speed. The thinner the armor, or without armor at all, the faster and better able the ship was to run away from a more powerful enemy; but with little or no armor, it was also unable to thwart the tactical objectives of an enemy. Any reasonably balanced fleet— that is, a fleet comprising a sufficient variety of necessary types to offer a commander a choice of tactical options—would require that some ships with each capability be included. A ship that was a half-way compromise would be useless, as it could neither run away from nor catch up with an enemy.

The recognized categories of warship design which at one time or another during the last fifteen years of the century the United States was to experiment with, and the representative characteristics of each (although not necessarily descriptive of contemporaneous U.S. Navy ships), were these:

BATTLESHIP. The most powerful of all warships, it was assigned the primary mission of attacking an enemy battle fleet. Large (up to 15,000 tons' displacement) and heavily armored (8 to 24 inches of wrought iron, steel, or a combination of the two), the battleship mounted a main battery with guns as large as the 16.25-inch type, and many guns of smaller size. Speed was limited to about 18 knots, but a battleship did not have to be able to run away from a fight. The battleship became the one accepted symbol of naval power throughout the world; and, because of both the strategic and diplomatic implications inherent in a ship of such aggressive potential, it became the most controversial and publicly discussed type of ship in the United States.

ARMORED CRUISER. Often larger than a battleship, the armored cruiser had lighter armor protection and a main battery of six or eight 8-inch guns. Firepower was supplemented by numerous smaller guns, but was considerably below that of the battleship. The virtue of the armored cruiser was its high speed (24 knots) and its vastly

[9]

extended cruising range (endurance as high as 25,000 miles).

PROTECTED CRUISER. With a displacement of up to 5,000 tons, the protected cruiser carried an armored deck several inches thick, but no side armor. It usually mounted one or two 8-inch guns, as well as the expected smaller guns. Its maximum speed was about 20 knots. The first five cruisers of the "new Navy," those authorized in 1883 and 1885, were of this type.

UNPROTECTED CRUISER. Slightly smaller than the protected cruiser, with a main battery no larger than the 5-inch gun, this type of ship relied upon its watertight compartmentation, peripheral coal bunkers, and a hull packing of either cocoa fiber or cornstalk pith (which would swell up when wet, theoretically blocking the entrance of any more water into the hull) for protection against battle damage.

DESTROYER. Developed toward the end of the century, the destroyer was an offspring of the "torpedo-boat destroyer," which itself had been developed from the torpedo boat. At first known by the clumsy title of "destroyers of torpedo-boat destroyers," ships of this and the smaller class came to be called, simply, "destroyers." Relatively small, with a maximum displacement of 400 tons; armed with torpedoes (which were also installed on battleships and cruisers until it became apparent that they would only rarely—if ever—be employed in battle) and small-caliber rapid-fire guns; and capable of speeds up to 35 knots.

TORPEDO BOAT. It was the most discussed, most feared, and least effective ship of the day. Small (85 to 100 feet) and fast, the class had been created to take advantage of the tactical benefits offered by the Whitehead automobile torpedo. In theory, the boats would move in on a more powerful enemy, preferably under cover of darkness, and, when within range of about 400 yards, launch a torpedo set to run just below the surface of the water, so that it would crash into the enemy hull just under the armor belt. Early development of such counteroffensive weapons as the searchlight and the rapid-fire gun, as well as the destroyer, prevented the torpedo boat from ever living up to its theoretical potential. By 1890, when the United States commissioned its first torpedo boat, the five leading navies of the world had a combined total of over 900 of them in service. It is unlikely that any of these boats ever inflicted any appreciable damage on an enemy.

DYNAMITE CRUISER. This type of cruiser was slim and yachtlike, mounting three 15-inch firing tubes that projected from the forward deck like so many ventilator shafts and were, from a military point of view, about as useful. Using compressed air as a propellant, these tubes were designed to send a 7-foot-long projectile with an explosive charge of 250 pounds of TNT for a range of 1.5 miles. In theory, an enemy ship could be destroyed either by a direct hit or sunk as a result of the underwater concussion of a near miss. The only ship of this type built by the U.S. Navy, the *Vesuvius*, never achieved any degree of success and saw scant and useless service as a dispatch boat. The only other dynamite cruiser ever built for any navy—Brazil's *Nictheroy*—was later purchased by the United States for use as a gunboat in the Spanish-American War.

RAM. Another nearly unique vessel, the armored ram *Katahdin* had a low, cigar-shaped hull with a pointed, semisubmerged bow designed to punch a hole in the side of an enemy ship. The ram was a type of ship more suited to the combats of the ancient Greek and Roman navies than to any modern fighting, but because ramming had been effective in several more-or-less recent battles, great importance was attached to the design. For many years, most major warships were constructed with great protruding ram bows. Like the dynamite cruiser, the ram proved to be useless; the *Katahdin* ended its days as a gunnery target. The only other ram of modern times was the British *Polyphemus*, laid down in 1878.

[11]

SUBMARINE. A radical design, a few submarines were being built in Europe for experimental purposes. The U.S. Navy was mildly interested and contracted for a prototype; but it was unsatisfactory and was not accepted for service.

DISPATCH BOAT. It was little more than an oceangoing yacht, lightly armed, providing a messenger service between units of the fleet and shore-based headquarters.

GUNBOAT. Averaging about 1,000 tons, these small ships were relatively heavily armed with 6-inch and 4-inch rapid-firing guns. They were primarily intended for use on inland waters, in rivers, or for blockade duty off an enemy harbor, thereby freeing larger ships for other duty.

MONITOR. The monitor was a class of ship derived from the original Civil War vessel, and something of a military hangover. It had been a brilliant innovation when first introduced and, as it was well suited for work in the shallow waters of rivers and harbors, it had been reasonably successful. The monitor was the favored type of ship for coast defense work, and for many years was the only type of armored ship to be built by the United States. It was also something of a political football, since it was cheap to build and yet warlike enough in appearance to be a comfort to any seacoast city and, by extension, a credit to the reputation of any legislator who put it there. The many champions of the monitor looked upon it as the ideal compromise armored warship and ignored the fatal weaknesses in the design that could never be overcome. Among the defects: a very quick roll—a period of under three seconds—that made it almost impossible to aim a gun unless operating in completely sheltered waters; extremely low freeboard (practically speaking, it had none) which meant that the guns were frequently half underwater in any seaway (although the low freeboard was considered by many to be a virtue because it would make the monitor a difficult target for enemy gunners); and dangerously low reserve buoyancy—

[12]

on the order of 20 per cent. They would, in other words, sink if they took aboard as little as one-fifth of their weight in water. Any respectable armored warship of the period had a reserve buoyancy of 80 per cent.

Useless though they may have been, the monitors can be credited with being indirectly responsible for the next positive step in the rejuvenation of the Navy. In 1886, Congress gave approval for the completion of four double-turreted monitors that had been planned at the close of the Civil War. The *Puritan, Amphitrite, Monadnock,* and *Terror* had furnished work for contractors off and on through the postwar years. Construction had been suspended after the war, started anew in 1874, again suspended in 1877, and recommenced in 1882. The hulls were finally launched in 1883, but work was again suspended. The reason put forth for this stop-and-go activity was that the designs had to be frequently changed to keep up with advances in technology: the armor became thicker; the guns became larger; the machinery underwent several modifications. The original wooden hulls had rotted away and were replaced with new iron hulls—and in the end, about all that was left of the original designs were the names.

The addition of these four monitors to the Navy was not particularly important in itself, but there was a clause in the authorization which was to have an important and long-lasting effect upon both the Navy and American industry. Congress—ever mindful of the welfare of American business concerns—slipped in a provision that the materials for these ships (which were to be completed "in a reasonable time") must be of "domestic manufacture." Since at that time there was no mill in the United States capable of producing armor plate, nor had one been planned, the phrase "in a reasonable time" was interpreted by the Navy Department to include whatever time would be necessary for the design and construction of such a mill. The first contract for domestic armor was awarded to the Bethlehem Iron and Steel Company in the spring of 1877, and that led directly to the growth of the steelmaking and munitions industries in the United States.

In the same act, Congress also authorized two new ships which, though loosely described as either "armored cruisers" or "second-class battleships" (they were both officially designated as the latter prior to commissioning), were the first modern armored warships to be built by the United States. The *Texas* was built from designs procured in England through a competition in which a prize of $15,000 was offered for the best design submitted. The *Maine* was wholly designed by American naval architects, eager to prove that the failures of the ABCD's were not symptomatic of any native lack of skill. She became the largest ship ever to have been built in a Navy yard. (Unfortunately, the *Maine,* too, had a few defects. When first loaded with stores, it was discovered that an error had been made in the loading plans, because the ship drew three feet more water forward than aft. Forty-eight tons of ballast installed near the stern straightened it up.)

Two years later, another major warship was authorized—the armored cruiser *New York.* Larger and swifter than either the *Texas* or the *Maine,* it was also well enough designed so that it elicited the open admiration of several European navies. They were apparently unaware that the basic design of the *New York* had been surreptitiously borrowed from one of them. It would be many years before American designers achieved independent maturity.

During the period 1881–88, authorizations were obtained for thirty-four ships in all, most of them of minor types. But the programs were a fair start and provided new ships to replace the worn out and hopelessly obsolete wooden ships of the "old Navy." The authorizations brought no radical change to the make up of the Navy itself, however; and, indeed, in the orthodox naval strategy of the day, no radical changes were called for.

But a revolution in strategic thinking was soon to come; and with it, a major change in the character not only of the U.S. Navy but of all navies throughout the world. And it was to be a decidedly American contribution.

[14]

TWO

⚓

Revolution

*An improvement of weapons is due to the
energy of one or two men, while changes in
tactics have to overcome the inertia of a
conservative class . . . a great evil.*
—Captain Alfred Thayer Mahan,
*The Influence of Sea Power upon History,
1660–1783*

IT WAS Secretary of the Navy Benjamin F. Tracy, assuming office
with the Harrison Administration in 1889, who gave the first public
indication that a new naval strategy was coming into being. Tracy
pointed out the vulnerability of the United States to open attack,
and decried the practice of building numerous unarmored ships that
would be practically useless in any combat. "The country needs a
Navy that will exempt it from war," he wrote in his first annual report, "but the only Navy that will accomplish this is a Navy that can
wage war." Tracy went on to imply the folly of relying on the "intelligence, culture, and skill of the people" without providing them with
adequate weapons in advance. "Naval wars in the future," he continued, "will be short and sharp. It is morally certain that they will
be fought out to the end with the force available in the beginning."

Secretary Tracy called for the prompt creation of a fleet of 20
battleships, 20 monitors, and a strong force of cruisers. A few months
later, a special Naval Policy Board which had been established at his

request, brought in an even more ambitious program. Recognizing the continuing growth of foreign trade, the need to protect shipping, and the strategic impact of a proposed isthmian canal in Central America, the board recommended a fleet of 42 battleships and monitors, 40 cruisers, 117 torpedo boats, and 11 rams. Actually, there was scant hope that this program would gain support in Congress, not so much because it called for an increase in the size of the Navy by some 500 per cent but because it based its request on the recognition of military principles even more advanced than those openly considered by Secretary Tracy. The board, discarding the traditional philosophy of harbor defense and commerce raiding, flatly came out in favor of a strong fighting force that could attack "points on the other side of the Atlantic." For the lawmakers of a peaceloving nation this had too much of the flavor of "aggression"; it would hurt the country's image abroad if it built battleships that could attack European cities. It mattered little that the United States had "a record of conquest, colonization, and expansion unequaled by any people in the nineteenth century" (as Senator Henry Cabot Lodge was to say a few years later). Indians and Mexicans did not vote in American elections. Neither, of course, did Europeans—but many of their children did.

Senator Eugene Hale of Maine took the initiative for the Administration and introduced a bill calling for construction of eight battleships, two monitors, two gunboats, and five torpedo boats. A substantial group of legislators—for the most part men who had long been champions, for whatever reasons, of the monitor—expressed horror at the thought of appropriating taxpayer's money for battleships. To appease them somewhat an alternate proposal was introduced, substituting a smaller ship than a battleship but with more freeboard than a monitor. Great emphasis was placed upon the idea that these were to be considered as purely defensive ships, of limited range, but so designed as to be capable, should the need arise, of conducting operations at sea.

Even this logical reasoning did not go unchallenged. "What is the

[16]

need for them?" an opponent asked. "If we become involved in war with any foreign nation, where will the fight be? . . . We will not go out upon the ocean to give battle. We will not go to a foreign shore . . . We are not thinking of foreign conquest." Of course, in the context of both the accepted naval strategy and a continuing national policy of noninvolvement in foreign affairs, this was a fair argument. It had not yet come to the attention of Congress that a reexamination of naval strategy had just occurred which had influenced the thinking of both Secretary Tracy and the Naval Policy Board. The implications of this would, within a few years, have a profound influence on United States foreign policy. This was the famous doctrine of "sea power" created by Navy Captain Alfred Thayer Mahan.

Mahan, a competent but hitherto undistinguished officer, had been assigned to deliver a series of lectures on naval history and tactics at the recently established Naval War College. In preparing his lectures, he evolved a theory of the employment of naval forces, in peace as well as war, that was to be his major contribution to the history of mankind.

Captain Mahan had once been an orthodox believer in "coast defense and commerce raiding," but his studies in history convinced him that any nation which adhered to such a narrow concept was fatally vulnerable. He urged the creation of a strong, concentrated naval force that could stop an enemy before a situation requiring coast defense could arise. Although his lectures were delivered before very few officers, and his noted book, *The Influence of Sea Power upon History, 1660–1783*, had not yet appeared, it is certain that his ideas were embodied in Secretary Tracy's request.

Briefly, Mahan's theories—which he was to further explore in twenty-one books and over one hundred and twenty magazine articles—called for a powerful battle fleet in time of war which could take the offensive against the enemy, and a widespread system of overseas colonies and bases. These would be supported by a strong merchant marine and protected by the Navy in time of peace; and

[17]

they in turn would help support the Navy in time of war. His doctrines, if accepted, were a franchise for enlargement of the Navy and expansion of United States power and influence to areas of the world far removed from the North American continent.

The greatest influence of Mahan's work was not, however, immediately felt in the United States; but it was widely accepted overseas, primarily in England, Germany, and Japan. Mahan was credited with being responsible for a £3,000,000 shipbuilding appropriation in England where interest in the navy had been waning; in Germany, Kaiser Wilhelm made his book mandatory reading for all naval officers; and in Japan, more of Mahan's books were translated into that country's language than into any other. It was not until the middle 1890's that Mahan began to receive open recognition in the United States, as more and more supporters came to accept his theories, especially those which called for colonization and expansion. One historian has observed, "It was not that what he said was profound, but that he had the luck to say it at a moment in history when countless prosperous and influential persons were looking for precisely this justification for courses which they wished for their own reasons to pursue."

Mahan did however have one immediate effect upon United States policies—a redefinition of terms that went a long way to clear up some of the muddled strategic thinking, circa 1890. For example, the phrase "coast defense" in and of itself inhibited imaginative planning. To most people, naval, civilian, and political alike, it implied the use of ships that would never be required to go out of sight of land—ships with heavy armor and powerful guns, but of light draft so as to be able to operate within shallow harbors. Such ships would also be of limited range, because extended operations at sea were not contemplated. In other words, a fleet of monitors.

What the monitor supporters failed to consider was that a monitor would neither be able to stand up to a battleship nor prevent a battleship from executing a successful attack. Since the monitor would not be able to put to sea to intercept a battleship raid, the enemy ships would have only to lie just out of range and, with their more powerful guns, fire over the monitor and bombard their objective without even having to acknowledge the "coast defense" ship's presence at the scene. The monitor supporters also took it for granted that an enemy's intentions would be known in advance, so that the fleet of monitors could be concentrated to repel the attack. Such an assumption ignored the possibility of the enemy slipping in to blockade a port, without warning. Moreover, monitors, in whatever number, would not be able to move in and execute a successful attack from seaward.

Debate over the Hale bill raged hot and heavy. Supporters of the battleship maintained that it would be shortsighted policy to so hamstring the Navy that it could never break away from the coastline; it would be far better to spend the money on versatile weapons that would be a match for anything the enemy could bring into battle. The battleship was held up, not as a tool of aggression, but as the nation's "first line of defense."

The opposition was adamant, but in its partisan fervor to put down an Administration-backed proposal it revealed itself to be completely ignorant of the situation. The minority report on the Hale bill asserted that the time had not yet come for the United States to build "unwieldly broadside armored vessels, which, with European nations, are experiments of at least doubtful value." This was an interesting point of view, as the proposed ships were neither "broadside battleships"—a broadside ship had not been constructed by any navy in the world for twenty years—nor unwieldly. The proposed ships would have their guns mounted in turrets and have a projected speed of 17 knots, which would have made them far more "wieldly" than the best of the monitors, whose top speed was 13 knots and whose low freeboard seriously inhibited maneuvering.

Former Secretary of the Navy Chandler, who could claim a certain amount of experience in these matters, was the opposition leader against the "broadside battleships." He offered a substitute program to comprise a fleet of monitors, small cruisers, and gunboats, and set forth some pretentious but rather silly reasons why his program was the better. At this point, a number of newspapers gleefully jumped into the controversy—it was not often that they had a newsworthy public figure who offered arguments which were so easily demolished. The senator had argued that the twenty-four-foot draft of the proposed battleships was "too great for our harbors." One newspaper was happy to list at least thirty-eight harbors in the United States—including most of the major seaports—that could accommodate, at half tide, a ship drawing thirty feet of water. Another paper, using Chandler's proposed specifications for his monitors, determined that the ships would have a wrought iron armor belt of 11 inches—thin enough to be penetrated by a 6-inch shell. Most major warships of the day were being equipped with 12- and 13-inch guns.

The New York *Tribune* had the most sport with Senator Chandler by confronting him with a statement that he had made seven years earlier while he was Secretary: ". . . we unquestionably need vessels in such numbers as fully to keep alive the knowledge of war, and of such kinds that it shall be a knowledge of modern war." The *Tribune* noted that the four major shipbuilding powers of the day—England, France, Italy, and Russia—were all turning out quantities of large, fully armored battleships, incorporating the latest developments in engineering and ordnance; and asked Chandler to explain how we could keep alive a knowledge of "modern war" by building obsolete and insignificant ships. Whereupon Chandler attempted to justify his position by listing four specific objections to the building of modern battleships. First, a "perfect" design for hulls had not yet been achieved; second, the question of which type of armor was best had not yet been resolved; third, advances in engineering were too rapid and the propulsion plants would probably become obsolete in a few years; fourth, guns had "probably" not reached perfection.

If Congress had ever taken such arguments seriously, the building of any ships for the Navy would have come to a complete and permanent halt. For this particular legislation, after all the arguments were in and all the politicians had sufficiently covered their partisan interests, the factions combined to vote authorization for the alternate proposal of a compromise ship, neither battleship nor monitor but somewhere in between. As an indication of strength of political considerations over military requirements, the vote in the House of Representatives was 131 to 105, and in the Senate 31 to 18. The House vote was almost completely along party lines, with the vote supporting the Republican Administration with the only deviation being by members with special regional interests. Of the 26 Democrats who voted in favor of the bill 24 were from seacoast districts where the Navy was considered important; 22 of the 23 Republicans who voted against were from inland areas where naval appropriations were of little political value.

The act of June 30, 1890, provided for three "seagoing coastal battleships," which worked out to be ships of about 10,000 tons' displacement, with an 18-inch armor belt, a main battery of four 13-inch guns, and secondary batteries of 8-inch and 6-inch guns. The compromise kept speed down to 16.2 knots, cruising range down to 5,000 miles, and gave the ships a draft of 24 feet, which appeased the shallow-harbor faction but did not seriously inhibit the fighting qualities of the ships. The *Oregon, Indiana,* and *Massachusetts* marked the turning point for the new Navy. They were considerably more seagoing than coastal, and were definitely battleships by comparison with which the *Maine* and *Texas* were little better than gunboats. And, while some of the legislators who voted for them may have believed they were upholding the image of a nonaggressive Navy, they had given tacit approval to the start of a shipbuilding program that was to add twenty-five battleships to the Navy in the next twenty years, and raise the United States to second rank among world naval powers. The congressional debates over the program, and the attendant newspaper publicity, brought in a secondary benefit: in the climate of increased public awareness of the Navy and its problems, Captain Mahan was able to find a publisher for the book he had prepared from his War College lectures.

The Navy Department gave top priority to the act of June 30, and in fact had the general plans and bid advertisements ready for issue the next day. Detailed plans were pushed through on a crash basis; bids were opened on the first of October. Two of the ships were awarded to a Philadelphia firm, and the third, the *Oregon*, was assigned to a San Francisco shipbuilder. The *Oregon*, because of its station on the Pacific coast, was later to prove both the folly of arbitrarily limiting the range of operation of a warship and also the ability of the Navy to sometimes rise above such operational obstacles. Because of their low coal capacity, the ships of this class were theoretically limited to operations within 1,500 miles of the United States; and this was precisely what the compromise planners had in mind. However, at the approach of the Spanish-American War, the *Oregon* was ordered to move from the West Coast to Florida, to add her strength to the Atlantic Fleet. It was a 13,000-mile trip around Cape Horn, and *Oregon* made it in a record time of sixty-eight days despite the fact that for most of the voyage she had to go in company with a coal-laden gunboat assigned to keep her supplied with fuel. (The previous record, set by the clipper ship *Flying Cloud* in 1851, was eighty-nine days, from New York to San Francisco.)

In spite of this demonstration, and in spite of other considerations, the term "coastline" was so politically potent that it was applied to all battleship authorizations until June 1900—even though designs which followed the *Oregon* class were not at all limited to short-range operations.

Of the four arguments put forth by Senator Chandler, only one could be considered to have any immediate validity—that concerning which type of armor was best for a warship. There were three different types available at that time—the standard steel plate, the compound plate of wrought iron and steel bolted together, and a new alloy made from 5 per cent nickel and 95 per cent steel. And in spite of the claims of the various manufacturers (all in Europe), no determination had yet been made as to the actual merits of each type. However, one was not long in coming.

[22]

When the Navy had let the original contract to the Bethlehem Steel Company for construction of an armor-producing mill, it had been understood that the initial production would commence by December 1889 and that the delivery rate would eventually reach 300 tons a month (equal to the output of the largest armor producer in England). But various delays were encountered, and by 1890 a growing number of half-finished ships waited for their armor, with no possibility of any deliveries until late in 1891. Someone at the Navy Department, making idle calculations, came up with the fact that even if the plant were immediately to start production at the contract rate, it would be almost six years before all armor for just the ships then under construction could be delivered. Accordingly, another contract was made—this one with Messrs. Andrew Carnegie, Henry Phipps, and Company (later called the Carnegie Steel Company), the largest steel producer in the United States—for the manufacture of armor for the Navy, at a rate of 500 tons per month starting by June 1891. And another heavy industry was unintentionally given a vested interest in the Navy and its programs. In future years, such interests were to provide a powerful lobby for progressive naval legislation.

But while the Navy was waiting for production of armor to begin, it was decided that it would not be inappropriate to conduct some tests on the three available types. As of July 1890 the United States had firm requirements for some 20,000 tons of armor for the twelve ships then under construction, not one pound of which had yet been manufactured. It was an unprecedented opportunity to equip the Navy's entire armored fleet with the most advanced armor protection.

A number of sheets of armor plate of each type were obtained from the manufacturers in France and England and shipped to Annapolis for the tests. The sheets were mounted on a firing range and, point-blank, one 6-inch shell was fired into each corner and one 8-inch shell into the center. The tests proved that the nickel steel was far superior—it had not cracked, nor had it even been penetrated effectively by the shells. By contrast, the steel plate, which had withstood the 6-inch fire, was broken by the 8-inch shell and the compound plate had been cracked by the 6-inch and destroyed by the 8-inch fire. The orders for the armor were amended to require that all 20,000 tons must be of nickel steel.

The *Maine* and the *Texas* were the first armored ships to be completed; they were commissioned within a month of each other in 1895. The *Maine* had been laid down first, and had taken over nine years to complete, three years of which were spent waiting for her armor. She was destined to have a short career—only two and a half years—but the *Maine* was also destined to become probably the best remembered ship in the Navy's history.

THREE

⚓

Life in the Navy

No other vocation gives a man such exciting and varied experiences as the Navy . . . danger . . . change . . . responsibilities . . . operations . . . and the continuous battle against the political influences that sap the strength of the nation.
—Rear Admiral Bradley A. Fiske, *From Midshipman to Rear Admiral.*

WHILE THE CONGRESS, the strategists, and the naval architects were busy planning the Navy of the future, there were some 7,500 men (slightly more than half of whom were United States citizens) who made up the existing Navy. These men lived, for the most part, with the concepts and equipment of the past. Day-to-day duties went on unchanged: watches to be stood in fair weather and foul; the ship to be cleaned, painted, and repaired; lines to be inspected and replaced and sails to be mended; new men to be trained. There were quiet months spent on tours of duty in distant ports; and the exotic, hidden places of the world known only to the seaman were visited.

Yet some changes were brought about by the rapidly expanding technology of the day. The living conditions on board Navy ships were becoming almost civilized, with the appearance of such luxuries as electric lights (on seven ships by 1890) and electric fans. The daily ration of food was made more varied as processing and preservation techniques were developed. Instead of the standard fare of earlier days—salt pork, bully beef, and weevily biscuit—the Navy man now dined on seven kinds of preserved meats, seven varieties of dried fruit, several canned vegetables, coffee, tea, cocoa, pickles—and had butter and molasses to put on his biscuit (which, unfortunately, was still prone to insect infestation). Also, since 1884, a portion of the mess ration was saved each day for distribution among the men on the midwatch, midnight to 4:00 A.M.

Other changes came with the growing emphasis on steam propulsion. There was a shift in muscle power, down from the masthead and into the fireroom where the backbreaking labor of shoveling coal into the boilers was a constant effort—it required 20,280 pounds of coal an hour, 338 pounds a minute, to drive a battleship at 16 knots. There were new rates in the Navy, and new skills in the fields of steam engineering, electrical engineering, hydraulic engineering, and mechanical engineering. And there was a fierce rivalry between the deck force and the black gang (stokers and engineers) that was not to be erased by any personnel legislation or directives from the Navy Department.

The old-time sailors were as critical of steam as were the senior officers. If steam was considered "dirty" by an admiral, it was dirtier to the men who had to clean up after it. When a ship was steaming smoke and soot covered topside areas; coal dust permeated the entire ship after a day of coaling (an all-hands job); and someone had to clean out and empty the cinders from the firebox. The smokestack of some ships was hinged at the deck, so that it could be folded out of sight when the ships were in port. It was not considered shipshape to have a smokestack cluttering up the silhouette.

But even so, the most recalcitrant of critics came to recognize the value of steam, as it began to prove its worth in a manner convincing to both grand strategists and the average sailor. The protected cruiser *Philadelphia* made a run from New York to Honolulu on one coaling and without using her sails. The protected cruiser *Columbia* made a record crossing of the Atlantic—just under seven days, with an average speed of 18.4 knots. The *Columbia* (commissioned in 1894) was the longest ship in the Navy, 413 feet overall, had triple screws, four smokestacks and—just in case—could be rigged as a two-masted schooner. The old school died hard, but steam finally made its mark. From the middle of the decade, sails were generally omitted from ships going into commission, but not in all cases. Some cruisers with auxiliary sail power were still entering the fleet as late as 1905.

As new ships were being designed and built, so too were new guns with which to equip them. Unfortunately, advances in the science of ordnance did not immediately provoke parallel advances in the art of gunnery, and no efforts were made to instruct the officers and men of the fleet in the care and feeding of the powerful and complicated weapons with which they were expected to do battle. A Civil War smoothbore with a maximum range of less than two miles, and the main battery of the *Texas* with sufficient power to send a 12-inch shell smashing through 26.7 inches of iron at 1,000 yards, were served in much the same fashion, using techniques that had been unchanged for nearly three hundred years. The gunner would squint through his open sight, or along the barrel of the gun, and touch off the charge as the target passed through his field of vision with the roll of his own ship.

Even though naval guns with ranges of almost 10 miles had already been built, no attempts were made to achieve accuracy in long-range fire because it was not seriously believed that the range at which naval battles were fought would ever exceed one mile. Later, when it became apparent that longer ranges would be employed, accuracy suffered because there were no methods available for determining the range of the target. Standard gunnery doctrine stationed a man high on the mast, where he could observe the splashes made by the fall of shot and call down corrections to the gunners. For ranges up to 3,500 yards, such spotting was reasonably accurate, and was helpful up to 6,000 yards. But beyond that range—at three nautical miles—the system was worthless. One enterprising naval officer recognized the deficiency and invented a number of devices to correct the problem, including a telescopic gunsight and an optical rangefinder. The Navy Department thought that Lieutenant Bradley A. Fiske had some interesting ideas, but was not itself interested enough to put them into service. Lieutenant Fiske was encouraged to manufacture and market them himself, which he did; his customers included some of the leading navies of the world.

Nor had naval operations changed much from earlier times. If a ship was needed for a specific mission, the Department would send it orders; but for the most part, the flag officer of a squadron or the commanding officer of a ship would determine his own movements, keeping the Bureau of Navigation informed by cable or letter. Schedules were practically nonexistent, and the majority of operations consisted of casual training and goodwill port visits, at home and abroad. The *Texas* and the *Maine,* as the Navy's first battleships, were especially popular visitors, and together participated in the Mardi Gras celebration at New Orleans in 1897. Their crews manned the rail for the King of the Carnival, and the *Maine* fired a twenty-one gun salute. It was a typical and successful visit, with crowds of civilians waiting in line for boats to take them out to the ships for a tour, and sailors waiting in line for boats to take them in to the beach. A good time was had by all, and the mayor of New Orleans put in an early bid for their return the following year.

Public interest in the new ships of the Navy was high, but people from the inland districts had little opportunity to ever see a Navy ship and were somewhat opposed to spending good money on something they did not understand. In an ingenious public relations move, the Navy actually built and manned a "battleship" on the Chicago lakefront for the 1893 Colombian Exposition. This ship— constructed of brick and cement on wooden pilings just offshore— was built from the early plans of the *Oregon*-class vessel and was christened, appropriately enough, the *Illinois.* In point of time, it was the first piece of U.S. Navy equipment to be placed in service and to be officially called a battleship, as it preceeded the commissioning of the *Maine* and the *Texas* by several years.

The more mobile units of the Navy were frequently sent off to some foreign country threatened with riot, revolution, or other internal strife, charged with the duty of "protecting American interests." It was not unusual for a ship to be dispatched without instructions or specific guidance. One expedition, launched because of troubles in a Central American nation, was enlightened only by a newspaper clipping that reproduced a letter from the U.S. Secretary of State to that country's minister in Washington, advising him that he was henceforth *"persona non grata."*

It was also sometimes difficult for naval commanders to determine just what might constitute a valid American interest. For example, in 1893, a revolutionary movement seized the government of Hawaii and deposed Queen Liliuokalani, while an American cruiser lent moral support from the harbor and additionally landed a few Marines "to keep the peace." The revolutionaries had counted on Hawaii being speedily annexed by the United States—this having been a popular issue in recent sessions of Congress—and there is little doubt that the senior naval officer present was in sympathy with their movement. However, when President Grover Cleveland was asked to sanction the proposed annexation, he was so horrified at the thought of the United States becoming involved in territorial expansion that he not only repelled the overtures but seriously considered using the Navy to restore the lawful government of the Queen. While Hawaii was disappointed, she rose to the occasion by declaring herself a republic and installing Sanford B. Dole, a prominent local citizen, as her first president. Under the impetus of the Spanish-American War, the Islands were eventually brought under the protection of the United States flag in 1898, when "territorial expansion" was no longer regarded as something repulsive.

Despite limited guidance and despite errors in judgment, Navy units frequently gave an outstanding performance in these often difficult assignments. John M. Hay, Secretary of State under Theodore Roosevelt and former ambassador to Great Britain, gave public recognition to these efforts in 1902 when he said, "I have always felt relieved when a naval officer has arrived on the scene, because he always kept within the situation." A typical example was the handling of the Valparaíso incident, when several U.S. Navy ships became involved in an 1891 revolution in Chile. Members of one of the warring factions were (unjustifiably) convinced that the Navy was materially aiding the other side, and resentment boiled over in the form of brutal attacks on Navy men on liberty in Valparaíso. Two sailors were killed and eighteen were seriously injured and, with feelings running high, units of the Chilean navy made threatening moves against the United States ships in the harbor. In this touchy situation, a combination of tact and forceful diplomacy on the part of the commanding officer of the *Yorktown*, Captain Robley D. Evans, kept matters from deteriorating. The Chilean government later volunteered to give $75,000 in indemnity for injuries to American personnel, and Captain Evans, who had resolved an explosive matter without fighting, became known as "Fighting Bob."

Another Navy captain, whose public fame was growing at the same time, was much too reserved to be tagged with a nickname. Then, too, Captain Alfred T. Mahan was something of an enigma. Naval officers did not write books, and writers of books were not naval officers. In fact, the consensus in the service was that Mahan would never amount to anything. In 1894, he was assigned to command the *Chicago*—against his will and over his protests, as he sincerely felt that his studies would prove of greater value to the Navy than any additional sea experience that he might gain. But the Chief of the Bureau of Navigation, who controlled personnel assignments as well as ship movements, was adamant in his belief that the proper employment of naval officers was on ships. Mahan went to sea, and quickly proved to his crew, at least, that he was a competent seaman. But, as luck would have it, the *Chicago* was flagship of the European Squadron, and the squadron commander, Rear Admiral Henry Erben, was not so easily convinced of Mahan's professional abilities. Not only was he distrustful, he soon became jealous of the overwhelming admiration that was openly shown to the internationally famous author wherever the ship journeyed. The admiral took every opportunity to exercise his authority, frequently interfering in internal matters of the command. Admiral Erben was also rather arbitrary when it came time to write Mahan's Report of Fitness, so much so that Mahan petitioned the Secretary of the Navy to convene a special board of impartial officers to conduct a full and formal inspection of his command. The Navy Secretary recognized the situation in which Mahan found himself, as he was well aware of the professional antagonism that was being shown to him by many senior officers. He handled the matter gracefully, ensuring Mahan that his official reputation was not impugned, and scheduled the requested inspection for the time when *Chicago* would return from her overseas station. The results of the inspection—which was indeed full and formal—vindicated Mahan.

It is of passing interest to note that, when *Chicago* departed the United States at the start of the cruise, the only copies of any of Mahan's books (he had by then published three) were in his own personal library, and apparently no member of the ship's company, officer or enlisted man, had read any of his work. As soon as *Chicago* arrived overseas, the ship's officers were besieged from all sides with questions about their captain, about his theories, and about the effect of his books on American naval planning. They could only mumble noncommittal pleasantries and seek to change the subject, until one of them located resumees and analyses of Mahan's work in *Brassey's Naval Annual,* editions of 1891 and 1893. The officers were able to get enough information from these volumes to at least hold their own in later discussions with their European contemporaries.

A naval career in the late nineteenth century was an interesting life for an officer. It offered constant change, travel, many friends, and positions of responsibility. The assignments were many and varied: in addition to duty on board ships, naval line officers served as instructors, inspectors, administrators, explorers, and surveyors. They might be called upon, in an official capacity, to provide advice on subjects ranging from naval tactics to home building (an officer stationed at the hydrographic office in San Francisco was asked how best to place a house on a plot of ground so that the living room windows would receive the most sunlight during the greatest part of the year). For officers with special professional interests, there were positions in the seven staff corps: engineer, civil engineer, naval constructor, pay, medical, chaplain, and professor of mathematics (with service at the Naval Academy or at naval observatories). The pay was not, by contemporaneous standards, too bad. It ranged from $1,200 a year for a newly commissioned ensign on sea duty, to $6,000 a year for a rear admiral (then the highest rank allowed); officers on shore duty, or on leave, or awaiting orders were paid on a somewhat reduced scale. There were always more applicants than there were openings, as the Navy was limited to slightly more than seven hundred line officers and slightly less than six hundred staff officers, in all grades.

But, while the work was varied and the pay acceptable, much of it was dull routine. There was little challenge; little opportunity for a man to distinguish himself, or even any reason for him to try. Promotion was based entirely on seniority. Outstanding performance might be psychologically rewarding but made little difference to the average career, and even sloppy performance had a minimal effect upon future opportunity. One commanding officer who managed to run his ship aground three times in one brief passage from Annapolis to the sea was not prevented from attaining the rank of rear admiral. Nor was another, who not only had difficulty in keeping his ship out of the mud but also was publicly censured by the Secretary of the Navy for failure to take any positive action when faced with a diplomatic crisis in a foreign port. And the censure was not mild: "In your apparent endeavor to escape responsibility," it stated, "you remained so completely passive that, as far as events . . . [in your area] were concerned, you and your vessels might as well have been on the other side of the world."

This same Secretary realized that there was nothing to prevent second-rate officers from achieving flag rank, and proposed that a solution might be found in instituting some form of selection process for promotions. In spite of his interest and the obvious truth of his comments, it was not for another twenty-one years (in 1916) that the selection-board concept was to be applied to line-officer promotions.

Another serious fault in the promotion system was that the ladder of advancement was jammed at the top with deadwood. Few officers chose to retire before the mandatory age of sixty-two, and as a result, in 1890, the average age of senior lieutenants in the Navy was roughly forty-four; the projected promotion opportunity for the lieutenants at the bottom of the grade, who were then thirty-seven or thirty-eight years old, was nil until they reached the age of fifty-five. From then on, they would have seven years of service remaining in which to pass through five senior ranks until retirement as a rear admiral —provided of course, that sufficient openings appeared. Officers reached command rank too late in life, after their health had started to fail and after their initiative had been smothered under too many years of subordinate positions. Neither they nor the Navy could benefit by such an arrangement, and Congress only reluctantly altered the grade structure to permit relief, by increasing authorizations for some senior ranks while reducing the number of ensigns and lieutenants, junior grade, proportionately.

George Dewey, unaware that he was soon to be catapulted into lasting fame as the naval hero of his era, had once summed up the career of a peacetime officer as he pronounced what he thought to be his own epitaph: "I will simply join the great majority of naval men and be known in history only by consultation of the records of the Navy Department . . . George Dewey, who entered the Navy at a certain date, and retired as a rear admiral at the age limit." Another officer, trapped in the rank of captain, urgently petitioned the Secretary of the Navy to see if a senior officer could be induced to retire. "My situation is a peculiar one," wrote William T. Sampson. "There are six officers above me who are younger than I am, consequently I can never reach the grade of rear admiral." The grade structure limited the number of rear admirals to six; but if Sampson had been able to look into the future, he would not have been so concerned. Within two months of this letter, with the United States on the brink of war, he had been promoted over the heads of several senior officers and given command of the Atlantic Fleet. This at least was one case where an officer's past performance of duty affected his promotion; and, because it was an unprecedented act on the part of the Navy Department, it was to cause a public and professional storm which did not die out for many years.

The source of all line officers, and the prime source of many staff officers, was the Naval Academy at Annapolis. The cadets (the term midshipman was not revived until 1901) spent their summers at sea on training ships, and the academic year in exploring the mysteries of mathematics, physics, celestial navigation, and other subjects considered to be of use in the profession. The course of instruction was supervised by line officers, but instruction itself was limited. Study assignments were given to the cadets, and they were expected to ferret out the information for themselves.

Discipline at the Academy was harsh, but life was brightened by monthly dances, and a visiting entertainer would perform three or four times a year. The cadets spent much of their spare time in unorganized athletics, playing for the fun of it. There was a football team: it practiced about two hours a week, with some mild sideline advice from resident officers who probably knew little more about the game than the players. It was quite casual in the days before the game was commercialized, and in keeping with the nautical interests of the cadets, the signals used in calling plays were somewhat salty. "Clear ship for action, by the deep six," for example, called for a kick by the fullback. This colorful system was abandoned when the Academy hired professional coaches, who found it too confusing. The first of the annual contests between the Military Academy and the Naval Academy was held in 1890, at West Point. Navy won. The team played under the new school colors of blue and gold, approved by a popular vote of the cadets over the former maroon and white.

The academic training took four years. When this was completed, the cadets were assigned to duty on ships of the fleet for a two-year cruise, at the end of which all members of the class were ordered back to Annapolis to take their final examinations. Those who passed the exams with sufficiently high marks were commissioned as ensigns; the relative scores achieved, when combined with the four-year academic record, formed the basis for the officer's rank for the rest of his career. Those cadets for whom there were no openings in the Navy were thanked for their interest, reminded that they had enjoyed a free education, and dismissed.

FOUR

The Tools of Empire

*I would regard a war with Spain . . . espe-
cially [from the viewpoint of] the benefit
done our military forces by trying both the
Army and Navy in actual practice . . . a
great lesson, and we would profit much by
it.*
—Assistant Secretary of the Navy Theodore
Roosevelt, November 17, 1897

IN THE MID-1890's, dreams of empire filled the political air. The abortive attempt at the annexation of Hawaii had served to whet the appetite of a small but influential group of men who believed that the future greatness of the United States must rest upon her position in international affairs, and who asserted that a country which maintained a head-in-the-sand attitude about the world beyond its own borders could never achieve any degree of greatness. But President Cleveland remained unalterably opposed to expansion, in whatever form. On one occasion, when some members of Congress tried to bully him into going along with a proposed declaration of war upon a neighbor to the south, he tacitly reminded the congressmen that while Congress might enjoy the power to declare war, he was commander-in-chief of the armed forces and could, if he chose to do so, refuse to let them fight the war.

But Cleveland was swimming against a tide, as was his equally peace-loving successor, William McKinley. They were bucking the pioneer spirit that had discovered the new frontier: the lush and profitable tropics and the corollary divine right of Americans to lead the more ignorant peoples of the world into enlightened servitude. They were bucking the ambitions of too many men in too-strongly-held positions; men like the senator who was not afraid to declare that "it is about time that someone woke up and realized the necessity of annexing some property. We want all this Northern Hemisphere; and when we begin to reach out and secure these advantages, we will begin to have a nation; and our lawmakers will rise above the grade of politicians and become true statesmen."

Cleveland would at least try; but McKinley would only talk about trying, while at the same time absorbing the eagerly pressed philosophies of his Assistant Secretary of the Navy, Theodore Roosevelt.

Young Mr. Roosevelt had already made his mark in the world. Elected to the New York State Legislature at the age of twenty-three, he had later been appointed Police Commissioner of New York City. He proved to be a tireless and aggressive worker, and was accordingly rewarded for his zeal with the Navy post. There had been several jobs to which Roosevelt could logically have been assigned; one of the President's political advisors suggested that, as an Assistant Secretary, "Theodore could probably do less harm to the organization." McKinley had his doubts—but Theodore was, after all, a deserving fellow. He got the job.

And he plunged into his duties with enthusiasm. Appointed in April 1897, he was by June publicly extolling the virtues of war. "Those who wish to see this country at peace with foreign nations," he announced in a speech at the Naval War College, "will be wise if they place reliance upon a first-class fleet of first-class battleships, rather than on any arbitration treaty which the wit of man can devise." The diplomat, he said, was the "servant, not the master, of the soldier." And the military virtues were vital to a strong country: "all the great masterful races have been fighting races."

This was by no means a new position for Roosevelt; privately, he

[37]

had always been rather militant. During a Venezuelan-British boundary dispute of 1895, into which—unwanted—the United States had thrust itself, as the great "protector" of the Western Hemisphere, he had written to his friend Senator Henry Cabot Lodge, "Let the fight come if it must; I don't care if our seacoast cities are bombarded or not; we would take Canada. The clamor of the peace faction has convinced me that this country needs a war." Roosevelt was a devout follower of Mahan, in whose writings he saw reflected his own dreams of an international empire for the United States. It is in a way ironic that McKinley, who would bend over backward to avoid any appearance of aggression, should appoint a man with such philosophies to the one department of the government where the tools, with which he could fashion that empire, were close at hand.

While it was in large part coincidental, the opportunity for Roosevelt to use those tools was not long in coming. A long-standing internal problem on the island of Cuba—90 miles to the south of Florida—brought itself to the attention of the American people.

This was a revolutionary movement directed against the Spanish government under whose rule the island had been since the days of Columbus. The movement had been at work for a long time, and had sparked abortive revolutions in Cuba off and on throughout the century, one of which lasted long enough to be known as "the ten years' war." It was not until the mid-1890's, however, that the movement became sufficiently organized and its operations began to have an effect. The members of this movement—most of whom lived in New York, New Orleans, and Miami, and had not been to Cuba for many years; many of whom had become naturalized American citizens—sought independence for the island, with themselves as the natural leaders of the new government.

One step toward this independence was to disrupt the economy of the island by burning the sugarcane fields; this had the desired effect of arousing the American business community which saw an annual trade of 100 million dollars being threatened. Since these acts were theoretically directed against the Spanish (even though many of the cane fields were owned by Americans) it was promised that, if the Spanish would leave Cuba, peace would return and trade would not be hampered.

But this was really a minor part of the insurrection, and served to keep people on the island apprised of the fact that a revolution was underway. Minor, that is, when compared with what was the most effective and best organized of the insurrectionist activities— and which was to provide the most tangible results. This was a propaganda campaign that put most of its effort into inventing and publicizing countless stories of horrible Spanish atrocities on the island, with the avowed intent of enlisting the sympathies and support of the American people to the cause of the revolution. While the Spanish government may well have been harsh at times, and while it undoubtedly used strong measures in its attempts to control the insurgents, it was not the obsessively cruel monster it was pictured to be. Nevertheless, the propaganda was highly effective; the insurgents always took the initiative, leaving the Spanish little recourse but to plead that the stories were untrue. American newspapers, ever eager for sensational material, printed everything the Cubans handed them. Indeed, some became so fired with enthusiasm about the operation that they started dreaming up stories of their own.

Two newspapers in particular (for their own private reasons) became the leading proponents of the insurgent cause. Joseph Pulitzer's *World* and William Randolph Hearst's *Journal* were at that time engaged in a massive and heated battle for circulation leadership in New York City, and each tried to outdo the other in finding and printing unusual items. Because of their size and the range of their distribution, they wielded an influence well beyond the geographical confines of New York.

It was a no-holds-barred battle, and has been described in sufficient detail in more comprehensive histories of the period. But one example may indicate the nature of the effort: the *Journal* printed an item that accused Spanish soldiers of conducting an "improper" search of a young Cuban girl on board an American steamer; to make the item sufficiently interesting, it was illustrated by a drawing from the pen of Frederick Remington, an artist of some reputation who had been sent to Cuba for just this sort of thing. The drawing showed the frightened, naked girl, surrounded by three lascivious-looking Spanish officers; and the implications were obvious. But the event had never occurred—at least, not as pictured by the *Journal*. The *World* did a bit of detective work and came up with the triumphant announcement that the drawing was a complete fabrication; the girl had been correctly searched by police matron, and the male officers had never entered the room. Both newspapers benefited by selling a few extra copies of an edition. The American public—which was getting fiction mixed with its news (and the fiction was remembered long after the news was forgotten)—was the loser . . . to say nothing of the Spanish government.

At every turn of events, the newspapers called for a war to clear the nefarious Spaniards out of Cuba. As time went on, as public indignation became more and more aroused, as the political expediency of having a war in an election year became more apparent (to focus public attention away from domestic problems), and in spite of sincere attempts by the Spanish government to improve conditions on the island and arrive at a reasonable settlement with the insurgents, the United States moved openly toward a war.

One important result of the propaganda efforts of both the insurgents and the American newspapers was that few people really knew what was—or was not—happening in Cuba. Most importantly, few people in the government were in a position to make realistic appraisals of the situation; and this included officials in Cuba as well as in Washington. The United States consul general in Havana, Fitzhugh Lee, was sufficiently out of touch with the realities on the island that he began spooking at shadows. In December 1897, he became nervous because it seemed to him that dangerous crowds of people were appearing in the city, obviously threatening American lives and property. So he sent off a request to Washington, asking that an American warship be placed in readiness to come to Havana to furnish tangible and moral support to his office. The *Maine* was put on alert at Key West, and Consul General Lee immediately contacted Captain Charles D. Sigsbee, her commanding officer, to arrange a signal that would serve to send the ship to Havana should the need arise. Like two children playing at war, the ex-Confederate officer (a nephew of Robert E. Lee) and the professional naval officer arranged a secret code: if the message "Two dollars" was received, the *Maine* would go on a two-hour alert; when the message "Vessels might be employed elsewhere" was used, *Maine* was to proceed at once to Havana.

On January 12, a minor protest action by some Spanish officers which did not affect American interests—and which lasted about an hour—startled Lee into sending the first message. He was soon satisfied that there was, after all, to be no trouble, so the second message was not dispatched, and the *Maine*—still presumably on a two-hour alert—was rescheduled to go back to New Orleans for another Mardi Gras celebration.

But the slight incident had been blown into a full-scale riot as reported in the United States newspapers, and they were pressing for action. Officials in Washington, who continued to be badly informed on affairs in Cuba, were uncertain as to what action would be appropriate. The State Department recommended that the *Maine* be sent on down, even though there might not be any immediate justification for it. The President was afraid that this would be considered a provocative move. But he was also afraid that, if no warship were sent and if United States citizens in Cuba were to be endangered, he could be blamed for having failed to take reasonable steps to insure their protection. Finally, a solution was arrived at: the *Maine* would go to Cuba on a "friendly visit," resuming a custom of reciprocal naval visits that had been suspended for the past three years. This "resumption" would be justified by an announcement that the United States government now considered the situation in Cuba to have improved to the point where the normal customs of former years could be reestablished.

Accordingly, the orders were issued to the *Maine* on January 24,

[41]

and Lee was notified of the impending visit. The consul general, with some misgivings about this plan, sent off a message urging a postponement of "six or seven days." But the *Maine* had already sailed.

In Washington, the Spanish foreign minister was not deceived by the "friendly" nature of the operation. Yet he rose to the occasion by announcing that, since courtesy visits were being resumed, the Spanish cruiser *Vizcaya* would shortly make a return call at New York.

The *Maine* arrived in Havana on the morning of January 25. While not exactly ordered to general quarters, the crew was on alert and the men were lounging in the vicinity of their battle stations. They had all read the stories of Spanish treachery. A harbor pilot boarded the ship, took her in to an assigned buoy, and she was moored. And the crew relaxed. The captain and officers went ashore for assorted official calls and visits. To avoid any incidents, liberty was not granted to the crew.

The *Maine*'s friendly visit was received in a friendly fashion, and after a few days the Navy Department—with an eye on the high incidence of tropical diseases in Cuba—was ready to recall the ship, her mission accomplished. By now, however, Consul General Lee had decided that it might be a good idea to have a warship in the harbor at all times, and requested that the *Maine* remain in Havana. The request was granted. The Spanish authorities were perhaps not very enthusiastic over this development, but accepted the situation with good grace; and life on board the little battleship settled into the dull routine of quiet watches and letter writing. The crew, at first excited at the prospect of going to Havana, now began to wish that the ship had gone to the Mardi Gras instead.

Meanwhile, Cuban revolutionaries in the United States chose this moment to play the trump card of their propaganda game. A personal letter of the Spanish foreign minister, written a few months earlier to a friend in Cuba, had fallen into the hands of the insurgents and was now released to the newspapers. While neither provocative, subversive, or illegal—it was, after all, a private and personal communication—the content of the letter was sufficiently disrespectful to the United States to cause a widespread reaction. Among other things, the minister had characterized President McKinley as "weak and a bidder for the admiration of the crowd . . . a common politician who tries to leave the door open behind himself . . ." However accurate the portrait may or may not have been was unimportant—the fact remained that the President of the United States had been insulted by a Spaniard. The minister resigned his post and went back to Spain. The American newspapers informed their readers that it was obvious that the Spanish government was responsible for its minister's personal opinions.

Had it not been for a more startling event that claimed the headlines, the newspapers probably would have been able to do a lot more with this theme.

At 9:40 on the evening of February 15, 1898, the *Maine* was shattered by two explosions. The first, a small muffled blast, was followed by a tremendous explosion that ripped through the whole forward half of the ship and, almost in an instant, killed 252 men. The ship settled rapidly to the bottom, and the confused survivors were soon either swimming in the muddied waters of the harbor or climbing into rescue boats. Surprisingly, there was no panic; Captain Sigsbee's orderly, Marine Private William Anthony, furnished history with a memorable example of attention to duty when, upon meeting the captain in a passageway, said, "I have to report, sir, that the ship is blown up and is sinking."

Three of the *Maine's* boats were undamaged and were put into the water, and other boats arrived to help in the rescue effort. Captain Sigsbee was reluctant to leave his ship while there was any possibility of rescuing personnel who might be trapped in the wreckage, but the fires were setting off shells in some of the magazines and it became impossible to remain aboard.

The captain sent an immediate cable to the Secretary of the Navy, both to advise of the disaster and to caution against speculation as to the cause. "Public opinion should be suspended until further report," he said, but he knew that he was whistling into the wind. The newspapers had gotten the news by 2:00 A.M., and the race was on. The *Journal* was quick to announce that the Spanish were responsible, citing no less an authority than Assistant Secretary Roosevelt. Based upon the reported opinions of "naval officers," the *Journal* was also able to graphically diagram the placement of the enemy mine that must have caused the sinking; but, leaving nothing to chance, Mr. Hearst also offered a $50,000 reward for additional evidence. Mr. Pulitzer dispatched a ship to Havana, carrying a team of investigators who were to uncover the true story for the *World*.

The Navy made preparations to convene a formal court of inquiry, and sent divers from Key West to retrieve the magazine keys and the cipher book, and to inspect the underwater damage. The divers reported there was a hole in the bottom of the ship; but none of them were construction engineers and were not really qualified to make any judgments. The Spanish suggested that a joint investigation be conducted, as being in the best interests of both countries, but this was coldly refused, as was permission to inspect the wreckage. The Spanish went ahead and conducted their own inquiry, using whatever evidence was publicly available.

A great state funeral was held for the dead of the *Maine*, attended by all of the military, civil, and ecclesiastical authorities of Havana. There was no question of the authenticity of the shock and grief displayed by the members of the official community, and the ceremonies were conducted with deep and sincere sympathy. Captain Sigsbee was uncomfortable at the thought that a Catholic ceremony must be read over the Protestant dead, but the tropical climate did not permit of delay until a Protestant minister could be located. The captain satisfied his misgivings as best he could by reading the Episcopal burial service to himself, en route to the cemetery.

Just at this time, the Spanish cruiser *Vizcaya* arrived in New York to return the visit of the *Maine*, the fate of which she had not yet learned. The *Vizcaya* was received with hostile silence relieved only by bare civility on the part of city officials who were, it must be acknowledged, more concerned that some overzealous patriot might try to avenge the *Maine* and give their city a bad name, than they were with maintaining diplomatic amenities. The visit was short.

Sincere expressions of sympathy for the dead of the *Maine* and their families were voiced throughout the world. The sincerity was somewhat strained, however, in some American newspapers, for which "sympathy" was just another avenue to good circulation. Hearst's *Journal* launched a fund-raising drive for the construction of a memorial; it was reasonably successful, despite the fact that former President Cleveland responded to the request for a donation with the following telegram: "I decline to allow my sorrow for those who died on the *Maine* to be perverted into an advertising scheme for the New York *Journal*."

There were a number of possible explanations for the cause of the sinking, but, somehow, they all seemed to point to Spanish guilt. The Spanish themselves could have planted a mine under the battleship, or they could have assigned it to a buoy which they knew to be over a mine. Or, local Spanish troops could have planted a mine without the knowledge of the government. But, of course, little distinction was made between the treachery of individuals and the treachery of the government. It was also suggested that the insurgents themselves could have blown up the ship in order to gain sympathy for their cause, knowing that the Spanish would be blamed. But even if the insurgents had brought about the explosion, public opinion would have held the Spanish responsible—they should have anticipated trouble and maintained more efficient patrols in the harbor. The possibility that the *Maine* had been the victim of an explosion of her own, through negligence, carelessness, or accident, found few supporters. And most of them kept their opinions to themselves; level-headed men would bide their time and wait for the verdict of the court of inquiry.

Secretary of the Navy John D. Long was one of these latter, even though he bore the responsibility of the Navy Department should it appear that the explosion had been the result of an accident or—even worse—a faulty design. On February 24, he noted in his private journal: "Our great battleships are experiments which have never been tried, and in the friction of a fight have almost as much to fear from some disarrangement of their own delicate machinery or some explosion of their own tremendous ammunition as from the foe." He did not sleep well that night: and thus the stage was set for a major scene in the United States' dramatic entry into the world of empire.

The following day, tired out from worry and lack of sleep, Secretary Long decided to turn the office over to his able assistant and go home to get some rest. This was just the opportunity Mr. Roosevelt had been waiting for, and he became a whirlwind of administrative activity—in the words of Secretary Long (who hastily returned to the office the next morning after being alerted by a friend), his precipitate actions came "very near causing more of an explosion than happened to the *Maine*."

The Secretary's journal entry for February 26 continues:

> He means to be very loyal to me, but the very devil seemed to possess him yesterday afternoon. Having the authority for that time of Acting Secretary, he immediately began to launch peremptory orders distributing ships, ordering ammunition, which there is no means to move, to places where there is no means to store it . . . sending messages to Congress for immediate legislation, authorizing the enlistment of a number of seamen, and ordering guns from the Navy Yard at Washington to New York, with a view to arming auxiliary cruisers which are now in peaceful commercial pursuit . . . he has gone about things like a bull in a china shop . . .

Secretary Long was able to rescind many of the orders issued by Roosevelt, but was persuaded to let some of them stand. Perhaps the most important—the one with the most far-reaching effect, and the one for which the Assistant Secretary would have given the strongest arguments—was not affected: the following cable transmitted to the Commander in Chief of the U.S. Asiatic Squadron.

DEWEY, HONG KONG. SECRET AND CONFIDENTIAL.
Order the squadron except *Monocacy* to Hong Kong. Keep full of
coal. In the event declaration of war Spain, your duty will be to see
that the Spanish squadron does not leave the Asiatic coast, and then
offensive operations in the Philippine Islands. Keep *Olympia* until
further orders.

ROOSEVELT

If and when the war should start, Commodore Dewey would have
all the authority he needed to carry out the specified operations,
without any additional guidance from Washington. It is superfluous
to note that the Spanish squadron in the Philippines posed no military threat whatsoever to the United States; it was simply the Spaniards' misfortune to be stationed near some desirable territory. The
Philippine Islands were very interesting, imperialistically.

By this time, the United States was fully and firmly in the grip
of war fever. The President, committed to maintain peace, was
steadily being pushed into war, and was unwilling to take any action
that might offend anyone. But the pressures to do something—anything—were great, and early in March McKinley had a bill introduced into Congress to appropriate 50 million dollars (a sum he
knew to be available from the Treasury without additional revenues)
for "national defense." It passed without a dissenting vote.

Since the United States was in little danger of attack from any
quarter, and the only current international interest was centered on
a small nearby island, one might wonder against whom or what the
congressmen were "defending" the country. The Army did not wonder; it took the wording of the bill quite literally. All of its 16-million-
dollar share was allocated to the building of seacoast fortifications.
The Navy, perhaps more politically sophisticated, did not worry
about such strict interpretations and began spending its 30 million
dollars on such things as the purchase of merchant ships for use as
auxiliary cruisers and the awarding of contracts for anticipated
services.

The deliberations of the *Maine* court of inquiry were completed,

[47]

and the findings formally transmitted to Congress on March 28. There were no surprises, but neither were there any indictments: "In the opinion of the court, the *Maine* was destroyed by the explosion of a submarine mine, which caused the partial explosion of two or more of the forward magazines. The court has been unable to obtain evidence fixing responsibility for the destruction of the *Maine* upon any person or persons." In the eyes of the American public this inconclusive but honest appraisal of the evidence was sufficient to endorse the prior conviction of Spain; and the report of the Spanish court of inquiry, which held that the cause of the disaster was an internal explosion, went ignored.

As for the *Maine* herself, she was to rest on the bottom for fourteen years; but in 1911, a cofferdam was built around the wreck, the water pumped out, and the hull patched so that the ship could be floated and towed out to sea for disposal. A second court of inquiry was called to reinvestigate the disaster; its findings were no more conclusive than those of the earlier court. In March 1912 the *Maine* was scuttled in 600 fathoms of water. The question of responsibility for the original sinking has never been answered, but the weight of modern opinion leans toward an internal explosion.

When the findings of the Spanish and American courts of inquiry were released, the Spanish—knowing that they were being backed into a corner—made a concerted effort to avert further tragedy. They agreed to submit the matter of the *Maine* to international arbitration, but this proposal was ignored. Further, they offered certain important concessions to the people of Cuba and offered to grant a truce to the insurgents. Pope Pius X offered to mediate the issues as an independent agency. The offers of Spain were flatly rejected, and that of the Pope denounced as "papal meddling" in the affairs of the United States. As a last resort, Spain offered immediate and unconditional cessation of all hostilities in Cuba for six months, if the United States would agree to refrain from aggressive action. Spain, in other words, was surrendering; but the surrender was not accepted. The United States was primed for a war, and a war it meant to have.

[48]

President McKinley went before Congress and called for a declaration of war "in the name of humanity, in the name of civilization." He asked for authority to "use the naval and military forces of the United States as may be necessary" to secure the full and final termination of hostilities between the government of Spain and the people of Cuba, and to secure a stable government for the island. The Congress voted four resolutions authorizing intervention, "as necessary" to ensure the freedom and independence of the Cubans.

The resolutions—just short of a declaration of war—were never officially presented to Spain. The Spanish government, disgusted and humiliated, broke off diplomatic relations with the United States before the U.S. minister in Madrid could deliver them. The Spanish resigned themselves to war, not a little perplexed at the actions of their opponent. "While pretensing a desire for peace, a decided disinclination to the annexation of any territory, the people of the United States had done everything in their power to foment the rebellion in Cuba and to make it impossible for Spain to overcome it either by peaceful or forcible means." Thus one Spanish writer was to sum up events leading to the war.

On April 21 the President ordered a naval blockade of Cuba, and the Secretary of the Navy selected Captain William T. Sampson to be promoted to rear admiral and placed in command of the Atlantic Fleet. Sampson was junior to several eligible officers, but was chosen for the post because of his reputation as a hardworking man with a lot of personal drive—and despite his reputation as an unfriendly, cold, and distant man with few personal ties within the Navy. Other men—warm, friendly men with many loyal supporters—were later to bitterly contest this appointment.

The first ships of the blockade took up station off Havana on the twenty-second; a nationwide call for volunteers was issued by the President on April 23; additional instructions were sent to Commodore Dewey at Hong Kong on the twenty-fourth. And on April 25, Congress decided to officially declare war on Spain. To keep everything legal, the date of April 21 (the date of the Cuban blockade) was set as the effective date of hostilities.

And so the powerful young nation flexed its newfound muscles and went to war with an almost bankrupt nation that had less than one-fourth its own population. It might not have been such a one-sided affair, however, because the young nation had not yet really organized itself for the war, even though it had been pushing for it for more than a year. It was not until April 15 that orders were even issued to consolidate the Army, units of which were scattered through various isolated posts all over the country. And, even when consolidated, it was not a very imposing force, equal perhaps to one-third of the number of troops that Spain had stationed in Cuba. Moreover, the American Army was singularly inexperienced in either large-scale or overseas operations. The most recent fighting it had done was in the Indian Wars, in which small independent units had been the fighting force. By comparison, the Spanish troops in Cuba had been in the field up to three years and were well-indoctrinated in the peculiar conditions of tropical warfare.

The U.S. Navy, thanks to seventeen years of honest effort in re-building itself, now had a core of reasonably modern warships. And, thanks to the energies of Assistant Secretary Roosevelt, who had persuaded the Navy Department to anticipate the war in arranging for the purchase or charter of almost one hundred steamships of various types and sizes for use as gunboats, scouts, auxiliary cruisers, transports, colliers, hospital ships, and other support ships, the Navy was prepared enough. While the Army was desperately re-cruiting men and buying supplies, the Navy was out at sea, ready to fight.

But it would have to fight without the further assistance of Mr. Roosevelt. He was anxious to be in the center of things and so "accepted" an appointment as lieutenant colonel of the volunteer cavalry—an Army job. Secretary Long tried to dissuade him in this, well aware of Roosevelt's value to the Navy Department; but to no avail. "He has lost his head," the Secretary noted in his diary on the day war was declared, "to this unutterable folly of deserting the post where he is of most service and running off to ride a horse and probably brush mosquitoes from his neck on the Florida sands. His heart is right, and he means well, but it is one of those cases of aberration—desertion—vainglory; of which he is utterly unaware. He thinks he is following his highest ideal, whereas, in fact, as without exception, everyone of his friends advises him, he is acting like a fool. And yet," Long acknowledged, "how absurd all this would sound if, by some turn of fortune, he should accomplish some great thing and strike a very high mark."

Years later, he was to add a postscript to that entry: "Roosevelt was right and we, his friends, were all wrong. His going into the Army led straight to the Presidency."

Roosevelt stayed at his Navy post for a few days after the war had started, and was then off to Texas to organize the cavalry regiment that was known successively in the newspapers as "Teddy's Terrors," "The Rocky Mountain Rustlers," and finally, "The Rough Riders."

FIVE

The Spanish-American War:
Operations in the Pacific, I

You may fire when you are ready, Gridley.
—Commodore George Dewey, May 1, 1898

CONGRESS had declared war for the express purpose of liberating Cuba from Spanish rule, and to help the Cubans establish an independent and stable government of their own. There had been no call for any other military activity but, as matters turned out, it was from a country far removed from Cuba and without any connection with Cuba or Cuban problems that the first news of American victory was to come.

Some Americans—most notably Theodore Roosevelt and his friend Senator Henry Cabot Lodge—had been eyeing the Philippine Islands for some time. The United States was entering the arena of international competition and, to those forward-thinking members of the government who had long since absorbed the teachings of Captain Mahan, the United States needed some overseas bases from which the competition might be directed. And, since the competition was becoming especially keen in the Orient, where the nations of Europe were busily carving up the territory of China into jealously guarded "spheres of influence," it was deemed fit and proper that the United States should obtain some territory of its own so that she might be in a position to influence the activity. As war with

Spain became more and more of a possibility, Roosevelt and his friends had noted with great interest that Spain held title to what could well become an outstanding advance base for the United States.

There was a parallel between recent events in Cuba and in the Philippines, although very few people in the United States were aware of it. An insurrectionary movement had started in the fall of 1896, but these revolutionaries had neither the public relations organization nor the political support in the United States as did their compatriots in Cuba, and the movement soon faltered. A month after the United States State Department had turned down a suggestion that an alliance be formed, in the event of war with Spain, the self-proclaimed Republic of the Philippines ceased to exist. It signed a treaty with the duly constituted government of the Philippines and, in exchange for a payment of 800,000 pesos, its leaders accepted voluntary exile in Hong Kong.

In the fall of 1897, Roosevelt saw an opportunity to make preparations for an American takeover of the Philippines. And Roosevelt was never a man to let an opportunity go unseized. The commander of the Asiatic Squadron, Rear Admiral Frederick V. McNair, was due for transfer, and the energetic Assistant Secretary took steps to replace him with an officer sympathetic to the expansionist movement. There were two men eligible and available for the post: Commodore George Dewey and Commodore Howells. The latter officer was a close personal friend of Rear Admiral Arent S. Crowninshield, Chief of the Bureau of Navigation and the man directly responsible for personnel assignments. Also, Secretary Long was known to favor Howells, and there was little doubt that he would receive the command.

But Roosevelt preferred Dewey. The Assistant Secretary, satisfied that Dewey recognized the importance of this assignment, advised him that in order to obtain it, he must have some important political figure make a recommendation in his behalf. This did not seem like fair play to Dewey, but when he said so, Roosevelt assured him that the Navy Department had already received similar appeals in favor of Howells, so that any such move Dewey might make would only be a matter of balance. Somewhat reluctantly, Dewey approached an old family friend who was a senator from his home state of Vermont. That same day, Senator Redfield Proctor called on President McKinley to make the recommendation, and was at that time assured that Dewey would get the command.

The President directed the Secretary of the Navy to appoint Dewey. Long, who resented outside interference in departmental matters, considered that the commodore had acted improperly in this instance and called him in to demand an explanation. Dewey was amazed at Long's reaction; he told the Secretary that he was only acting in self-defense as he had understood that Howells was bringing political pressures to influence the choice. Long coldly replied that no recommendations in behalf of Commodore Howells had been received, and terminated the interview.

Surprised and embarrassed, Dewey passed the next few hours rather uncomfortably; but then a fortuitous coincidence resolved the matter. Secretary Long sent word that he had just been advised of a letter from former Secretary Chandler, urging the appointment of Howells. This letter had apparently arrived at the Navy Department a few days before, on a day when Long was absent and Mr. Roosevelt was Acting Secretary. The letter had not, however, come to the attention of the Secretary until after his interview with Commodore Dewey.

And so Dewey was exonerated. But as a result of this incident—whether because of the animosity of Crowninshield who had been prevented from appointing his friend, or from resentment on the part of Secretary Long—a traditional practice of giving the rank of acting rear admiral to any commodore in command of an overseas squadron, was broken. Dewey was personally instructed by the Secretary that he would not be afforded this privilege, although no reason was given.

As soon as he had received his orders, Dewey plunged into a study of all available material on the Philippines—of which there was not a great deal. The most recent material in the files of the Office of Naval Intelligence was dated 1876. But there were charts, there were books, and there was correspondence to and from the squadron. The commodore explored every detail.

He discovered that the squadron did not even have a full peacetime allowance of ammunition. A supply was on order, but the shipment was tied up in official red tape that no one seemed interested in cutting. Dewey was persistent, but was informed that no merchant vessel could be found to carry such a dangerous cargo. He learned that the gunboat *Concord* was then fitting out at Mare Island Navy Yard in preparation for joining the Asiatic Squadron; his suggestion that she be allowed to carry as much of the ammunition as possible was received with less than enthusiasm, but was granted nevertheless. Dewey made sure that this request was carried out by visiting the *Concord's* commanding officer while en route to the Orient. He impressed on him the importance of this cargo—to such an extent that the *Concord* postponed obtaining many items of normal ship's supply until she would arrive in Japan so that more ammunition could be carried on the voyage across the Pacific. In this way, almost half of the order was delivered. The remainder of the ammunition was moved fast enough when the Navy Department finally realized that it might be needed to fight a war; it reached the squadron just a few days after war had in fact been declared.

Dewey sailed from San Francisco on December 7, 1897, on a journey that was directly to result in the United States becoming a colonial power in the Western Pacific—and would place it, in future years, in direct confrontation with the expanding empire of Japan. The commodore's first official act, after relieving Rear Admiral Mc-Nair on January 3, was to request and receive an audience with the Japanese emperor in order to secure the goodwill and support of that increasingly important country.

The *Concord* was not far behind, and soon arrived at Yokohama. As soon as her cargo of ammunition had been distributed among the other ships of the squadron, all ships got underway for Hong Kong to await further developments. It was not to be a very long wait; in fact, the squadron arrived in port two days after the destruction of the *Maine*. Dewey began to make last-minute preparations for the war that now seemed inevitable: the ships were given a coat of war-paint, dirty gray to cover up the peacetime buff-and-white; minor repairs were effected, and stores were purchased from local merchants. The American consul at Manila, Oscar F. Williams, was contacted and asked to provide all possible information concerning the Spanish fleet, fortifications, and minefields.

The most critical problem facing the squadron, once hostilities had been declared, was that of obtaining needed supplies, such as coal and provisions. Under the international laws of war, neutral nations were prohibited from furnishing support to belligerents; otherwise they sacrificed their neutrality. Once a war had begun, the only supplies or repairs which could be obtained by a warship of a belligerent nation would be those sufficient to carry the ship only to the nearest port controlled by its own government.

Realizing this situation, the Navy Department authorized Dewey to purchase coal from any possible source while he was still able to do so. Since the local supply of good coal was exhausted (and the quality of the coal had a direct and important relationship on the efficiency of the boilers), the commodore ordered coal from England—and then purchased the ship that brought it, the steamer *Nanshan*. He purchased another, smaller, vessel to augment his force, the steam packet *Zafiro*. The Navy Department also directed him to enlist, if possible, the crews of the ships into the Navy for a period of one year, and detail an officer to assume command of each ship. But Dewey had a more sensible approach: if he had carried out the Department's instructions, the ships would have assumed the status of warships and thus have been subject to the prohibitions of the neutrality laws. By leaving them as merchant ships, with their original crews, he would have a free hand to send them into any available port as necessary. One officer and four men were detailed to each ship to act as consultants on matters of naval tactics and signals, permitting efficient communications between all ships of the force while underway.

At this point, Dewey's Asiatic Squadron consisted of the flagship *Olympia*, a protected cruiser which had been scheduled for rotation back to the States but remained on station in accordance with the orders Roosevelt had sent; the protected cruiser *Boston;* the unprotected cruiser *Raleigh* (which had been sent from the Mediterranean only a few days earlier); the gunboats *Concord* and *Petrel;* the paddlewheel steamer *Monocacy;* and the *Nanshan* and *Zafiro.* The *Monocacy* was detailed to Shanghai to investigate the supply situation and to make arrangements for use of some convenient Chinese harbor should hostilities begin. The central Chinese government was beset by too many internal (and external) problems to be able to interfere with any arrangements made by local officials.

This force was soon increased by the arrival of the revenue cutter *McCulloch,* which had been en route from Suez to San Francisco and was diverted to join Dewey, and the protected cruiser *Baltimore,* coming from the United States and bringing the remainder of the squadron's ammunition. The *Baltimore* also brought a relief for the commanding officer of the *Boston* but, with a battle in the offing, it was decided to delay the change of command. The spare captain was assigned to act as Dewey's chief of staff.

The *Baltimore* arrived in Hong Kong on April 22, after the effective commencement of hostilities but before the formal declaration of war, and was badly in need of repairs after her 7,000-mile voyage. Dewey had anticipated this need, and had arranged for a drydock to be empty and ready to receive her. The *Baltimore* was immediately docked for bottom-cleaning and painting. On the next day, the twenty-third, Dewey was notified by the British authorities at Hong Kong that hostilities between the United States and Spain had commenced, and that, accordingly, his squadron would have to leave Hong Kong within forty-eight hours. On April 24, he shifted most of the ships to anchorages in Mirs Bay,

[57]

Chinese territory some 30 miles from the British colony; and as soon as work was completed on the *Baltimore,* on the twenty-fifth, the rest of the squadron joined them. The British at Hong Kong viewed their leaving with sincere regret: the consensus was that the Americans were headed toward certain defeat.

The ammunition supply that had been carried on the *Baltimore* was then distributed, but the shortage of ammunition was to remain a serious problem. Even with this addition, the squadron was only carrying about 60 per cent of magazine capacity. Other preparations for battle were made; all unnecessary wood, canvas, and other combustible material was stripped from the ships.

In order to receive cables from Washington, Dewey chartered a tugboat and assigned an ensign to remain in Hong Kong to coordinate any communications. At 7:00 P.M., on April 25, the following cable was delivered:

> War has commenced between the United States and Spain. Proceed at once to Philippine Islands. Commence operations particularly against the Spanish fleet. You must capture vessels or destroy. Use utmost endeavor.
>
> LONG

(Although the language sounds like vintage Roosevelt, this message was actually written by Rear Admiral Crowninshield, at the request of the President, during a White House conference. Secretary Long was out of town, but returned in time to see the text before the message was sent.)

The squadron was ready; but Dewey was still lacking some vital information on the Spanish forces, and expected the momentary arrival from Manila of Consul Williams. That official had been sending along bits of information to Dewey during the nine weeks that the squadron had been in Hong Kong. In addition, officers of the squadron, posing as tourists, had been systematically checking with travelers entering from Manila and had received some data. But much of this was patently false, and had been planted by the Spaniards. Moreover, the sudden influx of American "tourists" was not very deceptive.

Williams arrived late in the morning of the twenty-seventh and brought word that the enemy ships had shifted from Manila to Subic Bay, a deepwater protected harbor about 40 miles northeast of Manila. By 2:00 P.M., the American squadron was underway for the Philippines.

While Dewey's estimates of the strength of the Spanish forces, based upon the information he had been able to gather, were not very accurate, they would have to suffice. The Spanish squadron under the command of Rear Admiral Patricio Montojo y Pasarón was known to consist of at least seven cruisers, and there were believed to be a large number of gunboats and torpedo boats also stationed in the islands. Rumors reaching Hong Kong indicated that the entrances to Manila Bay had been well mined, and that both the mouth of the bay and the city itself were known to be covered by extensive heavy shore batteries. Dewey's only comfort was the knowledge that the Spanish cruisers were old and that, insofar as could be determined, the four United States cruisers were individually the superior in size, speed, and armament.

The passage from Hong Kong to Luzon, the principal island of the Philippines, was pleasant enough—the weather was fair, the skies clear and sunny, the seas calm. The men of the squadron spent much of their time in drills and training, and in wondering about the outcome of this voyage. Few of them had ever had any experience in battle; and few of them had any understanding of the issues involved in war. The hysteria of the American newspapers had not completely penetrated to the far reaches of the Western Pacific, although some copies of papers were seen and read and discussed. But the news—the important news—had reached the men. They knew about the *Maine* and they were ready for a fight.

As the squadron approached the west coast of Luzon on April 30, the *Boston* and the *Concord* were dispatched to reconnoiter Subic Bay. They discovered that the Spanish ships had returned to Manila, and they also learned that the Spanish had been issuing some good propaganda of their own—at least in the Philippines. In a copy of a Manila newspaper, dated April 23, they found an ambitious proclamation by the governor general of the Islands. It started by calling Americans "infamous cowards who burn towns, pillage churches, sack convents, torture prisoners, and kill women and children," and continued in the following rhetorical fashion:

> The North American people, constituted of all social excrescences, have exhausted our patience and provoked war with their perfidious machinations, with their acts of treachery and their outrages against the law of nations and international conventions. The struggle will be short and decisive. The God of victories will give us one as brilliant as the justice of our cause demands. A squadron manned by foreigners, possessing neither instruction nor discipline, is preparing to come to this archipelago with the ruffianly intention of robbing us of all that means life, honor, and liberty. Filipinos, prepare for the struggle. And, united under the glorious Spanish flag which is ever covered with laurels, let us fight with conviction and victory will crown our efforts.

When the *Boston* reported that the enemy ships were not at Subic, Dewey had all of his captains assemble on the flagship for a short briefing. Since the Spanish ships had gone back to Manila, the American ships would follow them. They would enter Manila Bay that night, to lessen the danger from the shore batteries. The battle orders were simple: "Follow the motions and signals of the flagship."

The squadron cruised slowly out at sea until dusk; as darkness fell, the ships turned toward the bay. It was a hot and stifling night; the air was momentarily freshened by a slight shower, but it passed quickly. The moon shone softly through a slight haze. The ships proceeded quietly, all lights extinguished, all hands at their battle stations.

There are two main channels, each several miles wide, which give entrance into Manila Bay. The channels are separated by Corregidor

Island, and were at that time guarded by batteries of heavy guns mounted on both Corregidor and another small island, El Fraile. Information gathered in Hong Kong had indicated that both entrances were heavily mined, and that it was compulsory for inward bound ships to take on a pilot in order to negotiate cleared channels through the minefield. This information could have been true, or it could have been a plant; Dewey made a decision to ignore it and boldly force the deepest of the two entrance channels. He reasoned that even if mines had been placed there, the water was too deep and the current too swift to permit efficient mining operations.

At about ten minutes after midnight, a patch of flame belched from the smokestack of the *McCulloch* just as she was passing El Fraile. The Spanish battery opened fire with a shot that passed between two other ships. Four of the American ships began to return the fire, but only a few rounds were sent off. There was little point in wasting valuable ammunition on a rock that was quickly dropping out of range. In the engine room of the *McCulloch*, the temperature was about 170 degrees; it was at this time that her chief engineer, "a very stout man who took little or no exercise," collapsed from the heat. He soon died of a heart attack; his was to be the only American life lost in the entire day's operation.

There were seventeen Spanish guns, ranging in size from 4.7 inches to 8 inches, mounted on Corregidor and El Fraile. It was later discovered that the progress of the squadron had been followed since the ships had been 10 miles out to sea; even in the darkness, the squadron could be plainly seen as it steamed past the islands. For some unknown and extraordinary reason, the commanding officer of the Corregidor battery never gave the order to open fire.

The American ships proceeded at a speed of 4 knots, timing the advance to cover the 26 miles through the bay in order to arrive off the city of Manila just at daylight. Coffee was served around to the men at their battle stations at 4:00 A.M.; just before 5:00 A.M., the sky began to lighten with all the glory of a tropical dawn. The hills behind the city, smoky blue in the morning light, reminded the commodore of the hills back home in Vermont. The squadron approached the normal anchorage area in front of the city.

At five o'clock, the *Nanshan, Zafiro,* and the *McCulloch* were detached and sent to an anchorage out near some other merchant ships; and the signal "prepare for action" was hoisted.

But no enemy men-of-war were in sight. Dewey had expected to meet the Spanish fleet at this spot because the anchorages were well covered by the Manila shore batteries. The American ships swung slowly around in front of the city; at 5:05, three of the batteries opened fire, without effect, and four shells were fired in return. But the American ships stopped this exchange a moment later when the Spanish squadron was at last sighted in the growing light of morning. They were anchored further around the curve of the bay, away from the city, just off Cavite.

Dewey had his ships in column, 400 yards between ships, with the *Olympia* in the lead, followed by the *Baltimore, Raleigh, Petrel, Concord,* and *Boston.* When the enemy was located, the spacing was closed to 200 yards—about two ships' lengths—and the column headed for the Spanish squadron at a speed of 8 knots. The batteries at Manila continued their ineffective fire, and the batteries at Cavite and the guns on the Spanish ships opened fire from an extreme range at about 5:15. Two mines were seen to explode in the water about two miles ahead of the *Olympia,* possibly detonated from the shore.

Dewey calmly held his fire until he was certain that his ships had reached an effective range. At about 5:40, he turned to the commanding officer of the flagship and announced, "You may fire when you are ready, Gridley."

Captain Gridley had been ready for some time, and he immediately gave the order. The first gun to fire was one of the forward 8-inch battery; the range was 5,000 yards. Soon all guns on all ships had joined in.

Dewey's ship was headed for the enemy on a slightly converging course, and the range closed to a minimum of 2,000 yards, with each American ship firing to port as it steamed past the Spaniards. After completing one pass, the column swung around and headed back past the enemy, this time firing to starboard. Neither force was using smokeless powder, and the clouds of black smoke rising around them cut effective visibility to a bare minimum. Yet the shells continued flying in both directions.

Soon the American squadron was making its fifth pass on the Spanish ships which, except for an abortive attempt by one of them to ram the *Olympia*, had remained at anchor throughout the action thus far. However, at 7:35, Dewey received a chilling report: there were only fifteen rounds per gun of 5-inch ammunition remaining on the flagship—a two-minute supply at maximum rate of fire. The ammunition problem had been one of his biggest worries; and now, the thought of his ships being without ammunition in a hostile region 7,000 miles from the nearest source of replenishment, and without having inflicted any visible serious damage on the enemy, was indeed disturbing. Dewey immediately ordered the squadron to withdraw toward the center of the bay to redistribute their ammunition and consider their position.

However, as the American ships were pulling away from the battle and the smoke cleared, it became apparent that the Spaniards were in trouble. The ships were on fire, and the sound of exploding ammunition carried across the calm waters. The guns on the Spanish ships were silent. Also, the commodore soon received a reassuring correction to the report on the ammunition supply: it should have been that only fifteen rounds per gun had been fired, rather than that many were remaining.

At this point, since the Spanish were obviously busy with their own problems, and since the American sailors had been at their posts for ten hours, Dewey decided that this would be a good opportunity to serve breakfast and allow a short rest. He called for all commanding officers to report to the *Olympia*; he wanted to assess the damage to his squadron.

The captains brought with them the incredible information that not a single man had been killed in the action, and only two officers and six men had been wounded—all on *Baltimore* as a result of one hit. None of the other ships had been significantly damaged; it was later estimated that all the damage could be repaired for about $5,000. At the same time, although as yet this was unknown to Dewey, almost four hundred Spanish sailors had been killed and most of their ships were sinking.

The Americans returned to the battle shortly after eleven o'clock, but there was no battle left to fight. Only one Spanish ship was able to return fire, and it was quickly silenced. After a few smaller auxiliary ships which had remained out of the fight had been captured, the battle was over. The commodore described the entire event in one laconic entry in his diary, dated May 1, 1898: "Reached Manila at daylight. Immediately engaged the Spanish ships and batteries at Cavite; destroyed eight of the former, including the *Reina Cristina* and the *Castilla*. Anchored at noon off Manila."

As the ships of the squadron came to anchor, back before the city, the shore batteries fell silent. Then Dewey sent a message to the Spanish captain general, by way of the master of a British merchant ship anchored in the bay, stating that if another shot were fired from those batteries, the American ships would destroy the city. Also, he added that if there were any torpedo boats in the vicinity they must be surrendered (one had earlier made a brief attempt to attack, during the battle, but had been repulsed); and, that if the Americans were allowed to transmit messages by the cable to Hong Kong which terminated at Manila, the Spanish would be permitted continued use of the cable.

The Spanish reply gave assurance that the forts would be used only in self-defense; that the captain general did not know of the existence of any torpedo boats but that he would not surrender them if he did; and that he was "obliged" to refuse the request for use of the cable. After reading this note, Dewey directed the *Zafiro* to dredge up the cable—which ran through the bay—and cut it. Thus ended rapid communications with the outside world.

It had been a busy day for the Americans; a day of danger and anxiety. However, as the sun was setting, the *Olympia*'s band appeared on deck to play a concert of Spanish music for the entertainment of the hundreds of people who lined the shore, having come out of curiosity, to look at the invincible American ships.

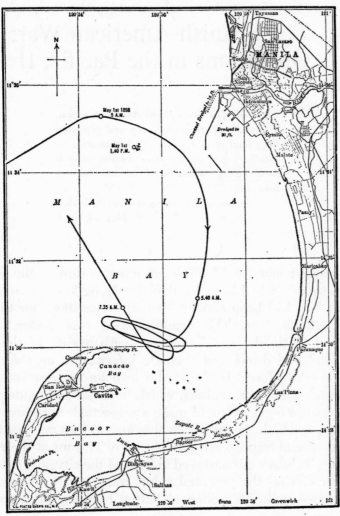

TRACK OF COMMODORE DEWEY'S SQUADRON DURING THE BATTLE
OF MANILA BAY

SIX

The Spanish-American War: Operations in the Pacific, II

*Filipinos: The great North American nation,
the cradle of genuine liberty and therefore
the friend of our people . . . has come to us
manifesting a protection as decisive as it is
undoubtedly disinterested toward our in-
habitants . . .*

—Emilio Aguinaldo, insurgent leader,
May 24, 1898

THE SPANISH FORCES in Manila were not unaware of the fact that Dewey's squadron had been positioned at Hong Kong for some time, and that they had been making obvious preparations for the seemingly inevitable war. The Spanish naval commander, Admiral Montojo, had timely communications with agents in the British colony, and had direct and accurate information on the strength of the American force. In theory, his own forces were formidable: seven wooden and iron cruisers, which were old and inadequate by themselves but together could make a respectable showing; 27 gunboats stationed in the Islands, each mounting at least one medium-size gun; and several torpedo boats. There were 17 guns at the entrance to the bay, 39 heavy guns arrayed in front of the city, and three other guns near Cavite—the potential value, using a ratio developed by Mahan based upon his studies of battles between ships and shore

[66]

batteries, of 236 guns mounted on ships. And there were quantities of mines which could be planted in the bay.

Considering these facts, it is incredible that Montojo made no useful preparations for war. The gunboats remained scattered throughout the islands; the torpedo boats were hidden in a river; only a few mines were planted. Shortly before the arrival of the American ships, Montojo had taken his cruisers and gone to Subic Bay—deserting the well-fortified environs of Manila—because he thought the smaller bay would be a more defensible position. This reasoning was not altogether faulty, for Subic Bay is a fine, deepwater harbor surrounded by high hills, with a narrow entrance easily commanded by an island that lies in the middle. However, upon arrival, Montojo discovered that orders to mount batteries and to place mines in the entrance had not been carried out, and most of the guns and mines still sat gathering dust and rust in a warehouse. The few mines that had been planted had been surreptitiously pulled up again by the insurgents (they had renewed their revolution when Spain went to war), who opened them up and extracted the powder for use in their guns. Thus, as a result of the complete lassitude of the local garrison, what could have been a nearly impregnable position was a completely defenseless one.

The discouraged Admiral Montojo held a conference with his captains, and they voted to return to Manila. If they were going to be killed, they reasoned, it would be better to die in less primitive surroundings. In his official post-battle report to his government, Admiral Montojo stated his reason for returning to Manila: because of the lack of fortifications and the great depth of water at Subic Bay, not only would his ships have been destroyed but they also would not have been able to save their crews.

The Spaniards returned to Manila twenty-four hours before the arrival of the Americans, and took up the position where Dewey found them. Montojo had forsaken the protection of the Manila batteries because, he later said, of the probable damage to the city if the battle had been fought in that area. The battery that he did have available was useless during most of the action: the guns were so mounted that they could only take under fire targets at ranges greater than 2,000 yards. The American ships were often closer than that.

Furthermore, the Spanish fleet, which could have exercised any one of a dozen tactical options, apparently never considered taking the offensive and sat and waited for inevitable defeat. On the eve of the battle—when he knew that the American ships were approaching the bay—Admiral Montojo had journeyed into Manila to attend a reception being given by his wife. He returned to his flagship about midnight; some of his officers made it back to their ships just minutes before the first shots were fired. Not surprisingly, the Admiral was later recalled to Spain for a court-martial. He was found negligent in his preparations; but the court stipulated that, insofar as his conduct during the battle was concerned, he had fulfilled his duty "in an entirely satisfactory and courageous manner."

Immediately following the battle (but before the cable had been cut) the Spanish captain general sent a message to his government in Madrid to announce the action. "Our fleet engaged the enemy in brilliant combat protected by the Cavite and Manila forts. They obliged the enemy with heavy loss to maneuver repeatedly. At nine o'clock the American squadron took refuge behind the foreign shipping on the east side of the bay." He implied that the Spanish ships might have suffered some damage, but was not very specific; nor did he indicate which side, if either, was winning the battle.

Dewey, who may not have appreciated the importance of public relations in this particular war, was in no hurry to send off news of his victory. With the cable out of action, he would have to use one of his ships to carry dispatches to Hong Kong for transmission; and for a few days, he was more concerned with securing his position in the Philippines than in furthering his reputation at home. He had, after all, only captured or sunk a few ships and obtained one small piece of real estate—the Navy yard at Cavite. The city of Manila itself and the rest of the Philippine Islands remained in the hands of the Spanish army.

[68]

Consequently, the first word of the battle to reach Washington had come via Madrid, and was not exactly inspiring. People learned that a battle had been fought, but no one knew who had won, or at what price. Secretary Long expected to hear from Dewey at any minute, but the days went by without news, and tension in Washington mounted. At both the Navy Department and the State Department, men were placed on a twenty-four-hour watch, awaiting Dewey's report.

It was not until May 5 that Dewey finally dispatched the *McCulloch* on the two-day voyage to Hong Kong. Three newspaper correspondents who had managed to accompany the fleet into battle went back to Hong Kong on the cutter. Understandably, they were eager to get their stories filed as quickly as possible, but in order that the official dispatches would not be delayed, they were made to promise to wait until they had been given a go-ahead signal. The *McCulloch* arrived in Hong Kong the afternoon of May 7; the official reports were sent off; and the correspondents raced for the cable offices. One proved more astute than the others: instead of filing a lengthy story at standard press rates, he sent a brief bulletin at full rate, which took priority over material sent at the lower tariff. His newspaper thereby gained a couple of hours on the competition in printing a "first person" account.

It was Saturday morning in Washington, and at 4:00 A.M. the clerk on duty in the State Department was notified that one of the ships of the American squadron had just been spotted entering Hong Kong Harbor. He alerted the White House and the Secretaries of State and the Navy, and when the dispatches arrived everyone important was on hand to read them. As might be expected, the news of a complete victory was received with great joy.

As crowds of newspapermen filled the corridors outside of his office, clamoring for the official word, Secretary Long sat down at his desk and began to prepare a statement for the press. But Mr. Roosevelt—in what was perhaps his last pronouncement as an official of the Navy Department—took it upon himself to break the news. He was a man who well understood the value of having good personal relations with members of the press.

Dewey became the hero of the hour. The President immediately moved to appoint him an acting rear admiral, and on Monday a bill was rushed through Congress adding another permanent rear admiral to the Navy. Dewey was appointed to the vacancy thus created, and the appointment was quickly confirmed. In other speedy actions, plans were carried ahead to send troops for the occupation of the Philippines (no one seemed to be concerned that the Islands had not yet been captured), and a resupply of ammunition was loaded aboard the cruiser *Charleston* which was assigned to escort the first contingent of troops.

Meanwhile, back at Manila Bay, Dewey had established a blockade of the city. All merchantmen in the Bay were assigned to a specific anchorage, and all incoming merchant ships were boarded off Corregidor, informed that a blockade was in force, and were politely warned away. Only those carrying coal were allowed to enter the bay so that their cargoes might be purchased by the Americans. Current market prices were paid. A number of foreign men-of-war—British, French, Japanese, and German—began to arrive on the scene, ostensibly to look out for the interests of their nationals living in Manila but more probably to see what spoils of war might conveniently be appropriated. They were assigned anchorages, and allowed communications with officials in Manila.

Dewey also established contact with the Filipino insurgents, who were eager to begin extensive operations against the Spanish and looked to the American squadron for encouragement and support. The insurgent leader, General Emilio Aguinaldo, had previously gone to Hong Kong to talk with Dewey, but had arrived only after the squadron had sailed for Manila. It was not long, however, before he appeared on the scene to take charge of the insurgent military operations in the Islands.

The Administration back in Washington, uncertain as to future operations and now openly interested in obtaining control of the

Philippines for itself, cautioned Dewey against entering into any "entangling agreements" with the insurgents, and to take no action which might commit the United States to official recognition of the revolutionary movement. The admiral was most punctilious in his dealings with the Filipinos: his meetings with Aguinaldo were cordial, but kept to a minimum. The only assistance given was to allow the insurgent forces to take some of the captured Spanish supplies. Aguinaldo's men began an operation that was soon to surround the city and throw many of its residents into a panic. Too many of the insurgents had an ax to grind and they were not expected to be too selective about where they ground it.

Relations with the insurgents were only some of Dewey's minor problems, however, for there were more important matters to occupy his days. Late in May, he received word from Washington that at least three Spanish warships and some transports were reported to have left Spain, headed for Manila. The monitors *Monterey* and *Monadnock* were directed to the Philippines to reinforce the American squadron; however, with a maximum speed of advance of about 6 knots, they (and their colliers) were not expected until some time in August.

Another problem was being posed by the German warships, whose activity in the bay began to cause some alarm. By June 17, three large German men-of-war were in port and another was expected, making a force somewhat more powerful than Dewey's. Moreover, the Germans had exhibited a disinclination to honor either the spirit of the American blockade or the authority of the American ships to maintain it. A German transport arrived, carrying 1,400 men who were identified as "relief crews" for the other vessels. But the men were not transferred, and the transport remained at anchor. The commander in chief of the German Far East Squadron, Vice Admiral von Diedrichs, arrived with his flagship.

Since there were few German interests, and only one German commercial house, in Manila, there seemed to be little justification for them to have assembled such a large force in the bay. The only comment that Admiral von Diedrichs would offer, when queried by Dewey, was: "I am here by order of the Kaiser, sir."

At this time a report arrived that a Spanish force consisting of two armored cruisers, six converted cruisers, four destroyers, and some transports, was definitely heading east through the Mediterranean. Attempts were made—via diplomatic channels—to impede their progress by refusing them any coal in Egypt; but they were apparently well supplied for their mission, and continued on toward the Philippines. William Randolph Hearst, now trying to help win the war he had helped to start, sent a peremptory order to the European representative of the *Journal,* commanding him to block the Suez Canal by sinking some ships in the channel. This unilateral act of war against Great Britain by Mr. Hearst was not carried out; the Spanish fleet transited the canal, and on July 1 anchored off Suez.

Dewey had his own ideas on how best to handle this threat, and had sent off an urgent message to the Navy Department. "In my judgment, if the coast of Spain was threatened, the squadron of the enemy would have to return." The Navy Department agreed; two days after this suggestion had been received, it was widely known around Washington that a "new squadron" had been organized and would sail for an attack upon Spain. No warships were available for assignment to such a squadron, but the ruse worked. Within a week, the Spanish had changed their plans and the threatening force had turned back for Spain.

Thus a bold deception had solved one of Dewey's major problems. It took bold action to solve the other.

Five German warships had by this time gathered at Manila, and von Diedrichs established a headquarters ashore near the entrance to the bay. The German ships moved freely in and out of the bay, taking soundings, visiting the city, landing mail and supplies for the Spanish, and, in general, ignoring the presence of the American blockade. They repeatedly refused to be boarded by the Americans who, in accordance with the terms of the blockade, claimed the right to determine the nationality of all arriving ships. Irritated by all the

[72]

continuing violations, Dewey determined to make a point of order on this particular breach of protocol and sent the *McCulloch* out with strict orders to board one of the German cruisers which had been sighted reentering the bay. The *McCulloch* hoisted the international signal, "I wish to communicate." The cruiser turned away. The *McCulloch* tried to go alongside; the cruiser maneuvered to avoid her. The cutter fired a warning shot across the cruiser's bow; surprised, the German captain brought his ship to a halt. The cruiser was quickly boarded, then allowed to proceed.

The next day, von Diedrichs sent a staff officer to enter a formal complaint about this act, and to present at the same time a written list of fancied grievances. Admiral Dewey listened patiently, then grimly asked, "Do you want war with us?"

"Certainly not," replied the astonished German.

"Well, it looks like it and you are very near it; and you can have it, sir, as soon as you like."

After that, the Germans were more careful to observe the conditions of the blockade. Later, after the fall of the city of Manila, when all of the foreign men-of-war were departing (the Americans were then in firm control of the area and there was no longer a reason for the foreign ships to remain), Dewey made a courtesy call upon the French admiral, thanking him particularly for his strict observance of neutrality during his stay. The Frenchman returned the compliment: ". . . you must let me congratulate you, that in all your conduct of affairs here, you have not made a single mistake."

"Oh, yes, I have," Dewey answered, and pointed toward the German ships. "I should have sunk that squadron over there."

En route to reinforce Dewey, the cruiser *Charleston* did its part in the war effort by capturing the Spanish-held island of Guam, 1,000 miles east of the Philippines and hence somewhat out of the mainstream of world affairs. On June 22, when the *Charleston* nervously fired a few rounds at what later turned out to be an abandoned fort, the Spanish thought it to be a national salute and sent for an artillery piece to be quickly brought to the harbor that the courtesy

[73]

might be returned. At the same time, Frank Portusach, a naturalized American citizen and the only United States national on the island, loaned a boat to the Spanish officials to carry them out to the American ships and to bid them welcome.

The welcome was extended; then the surprised Spaniards were made prisoners-of-war. But they were as quickly pardoned, and sent ashore to convey a demand for surrender to the governor. The latter made of show of refusing the demand, and threatened to have Portusach executed if he had any communications with the American ships. The governor, however, was soon persuaded of the hopelessness of the situation. Thus 230 years of Spanish rule were brought to a stumbling end. And U. S. citizen Portusach, the only American national within a thousand miles, was appointed by Captain Glass of the *Charleston* to watch over the affairs of the island until a more formal government could be established. As for the Spanish officials and military garrison, they were taken on board the ships and transported to Manila.

At the end of June the *Charleston* and 2,500 troops joined Dewey's forces; three weeks later another 3,600 men arrived. The monitor *Monterey* steamed into the harbor on August 4; 4,000 more troops were added on the seventh. It was then thought that the American forces were present in sufficient numbers to launch a full-scale assault on the city, and preparations for it were made.

For some time Admiral Dewey had been conducting surrender negotiations through the Belgian consul in Manila. The Spanish captain general had indicated a willingness to capitulate, but when he suggested this to his government at Madrid, he was summarily dismissed and his authority given to his second-in-command. The new captain general was just as aware of the futility of the situation as his predecessor had been, but he was necessarily committed to at least making a show of a strong defense. The new official therefore advised Dewey of the following: first, he would not surrender unless the city were to be attacked; second, if the city were not bombarded, the Manila batteries accordingly would not be brought into action;

[74]

third, if the international signal meaning "surrender" were to be hoisted by the *Olympia* as the attack was being launched, compliance would be considered. Provided, that is, that the Americans would give their assurance that the insurgents would not be allowed to enter the city.

On the morning of August 13, a coordinated attack upon the city of Manila was launched by the United States Army and Navy. It was a peaceful attack, as such things go, and the only American casualties occurred in a sector where some insurgent troops, who were not informed of the secret plan, joined in the attack and forced some Spaniards to fight back. The *Olympia* made a token bombardment of an empty fort (outside the city), and then hoisted the stipulated signal. It was very quickly answered by the Spanish, who displayed a white flag. Admiral Dewey himself first spotted this reply, and he told his flag lieutenant to take a couple of signalmen and the largest American flag they could find, and proceed to the Spanish headquarters to replace the Spanish colors.

The detail went ashore in one of *Olympia*'s small boats and pushed their way through the crowds milling about in the streets. They entered the headquarters building—still full of armed soldiers—and, without incident, exchanged the flags. Thus ended the war in the Philippines.

Unknown to either the Americans or the Spanish, however, the war between the United States and Spain had been officially ended the day before.

⚓

SEVEN

The Spanish-American War: Operations in the Atlantic, I

The New York Herald today publishes the secret doings of the Naval War Board; the intended movements of ships . . . I am in utter despair about these newspaper men . . . they pride themselves on getting information which ought not to be made public, and then boast in the press that they have made a scoop which no other fellow has done.

—Secretary of the Navy John D. Long,
May 14, 1898

THAT FIRST WEEK in May of 1898 the announcement of Dewey's victory at Manila spread across the United States, and the nation cheered. But on the eastern seaboard, the cheers had a note of hysteria in them. The Spanish Atlantic Squadron, under the command of Admiral Pascual Cervera y Topete, was known to have departed the Canary Islands, headed west, and had not been spotted since. The residents of the eastern seacoast cities went into a state of panic.

Tension mounted daily. Numerous false reports placed the enemy ships off one or another major city, and the local citizenry descended upon their duly elected representatives to demand protection. "Members of Congress," Theodore Roosevelt was to note later, "who had actively opposed building of any Navy, came clamoring around to ask each for a ship for some special purpose of protection connected with his district . . . brought every species of pressure to bear upon the Administration to get it to adopt the one most fatal course—that is, to distribute the Navy."

The pressure was so great that the Navy, in fact, *was* distributed. Some of the best of the ships were held back from combat duties and gathered together under the sobriquet of the "Flying Squadron," a name selected to give comfort to the widely separated cities along the coast. It was positioned at Hampton Roads, Virginia. Additionally, a number of less-valuable ships—auxiliary cruisers, converted yachts, hastily refurbished Civil War monitors—were detailed to specific ports in an attempt to pacify Congress. For example, one of the monitors was sent to the strategically vital port of Portland, Maine, manned with twenty-one naval militiamen. Portland was satisfied, although Roosevelt cheerfully acknowledged that the monitor "would have been useless against any war vessel more modern than Hamilcar's galleys."

This panic was brought on by the specter of four rather poorly armed enemy cruisers and two torpedo-boat destroyers, at large in some 41 million square miles of ocean. Actually, the entire Spanish navy should hardly have inspired such fear. The enemy had *one* battleship—but it was laid up and never saw service in the war. It also had one armored cruiser, the *Cristóbal Colón*, which was so new that the main battery was never installed. At the end of the war her guns were still being manufactured in Italy. There were three other armored cruisers in the Spanish Atlantic fleet which, in theory, could either have put up a good fight or have been able to run away from one. These ships, however, were in such a poor state of repair that they could only be counted as little more useful than the remainder of the navy, which was a group of floating antiquities similar to those demolished at Manila. (Spain had made one attempt to strengthen the fleet by offering to purchase two cruisers from Brazil, then under construction in England; but the United States moved in and bought them first.) Moreover, the Spanish Atlantic force sailed off to war with such a ludicrous shortage of supplies that the ships did not even have any charts of American waters.

Against this sorry collection, the U.S. Atlantic Fleet could send four new battleships, one second-class battleship, two fine armored cruisers, and an assortment of smaller ships. Of course, equipment alone is not the only measure of strength. Mahan had once said: "Poor men in good ships will always be beaten by good men in poor ships." As it turned out, this was to be a war—at least in the Atlantic—where men of questionable ability aboard good ships were to beat men of no ability in bad ships. The U.S. Navy was to write a seagoing comic opera on the normally somber pages of history, with a plot line based on incompetent decisions and petty rivalries, and an obbligato provided by a series of orders, counterorders, and non-orders.

On April 21 Admiral Sampson was assigned to establish a blockade of Cuba and, accordingly, he massed his forces off Havana. A few weeks later, when the lack of information as to the location of the Spanish fleet began to promote a widespread uneasiness, Sampson decided to take his squadron to Puerto Rico, on the assumption that Admiral Cervera might anchor his ships at San Juan, the fortified Spanish possession nearest to the homeland. The eastward movement of Sampson's force was not very impressive: the battleship *Indiana* could only make 7 knots because of badly leaking boilers; two monitors—which Sampson was determined to take along—had to be towed much of the way, and the towlines kept parting. The squadron covered the 960 miles from Havana to San Juan in eight days, arriving on the morning of May 12—only to discover that the harbor was empty, a fact, it should be pointed out, that could have been determined by a brief reconnaissance by one fast cruiser. For gunnery practice, the fleet commenced a two-and-a-half-hour bombardment of the harbor. The fire was returned by the Spanish garrison, killing one American sailor and wounding seven. Another man died of heat prostration. The Spanish losses were undetermined

[78]

but included about twenty civilians who had the misfortune to be in the line of fire; but this was, after all, a war. And this, the first "major" engagement in the Atlantic, was exciting, filled with noise and smoke. (When the war had ended, and the campaign medals were being passed around, a small controversy arose over whether this had been an "action" or an "incident." The medal board decided —over the protests of Admiral Sampson—that it had been an incident, and did not, therefore, merit a combat citation.)

After the San Juan engagement, it occurred to Sampson that he had left Havana covered by only a few light gunboats and auxiliaries, that the main Spanish force was still at large and might be headed for Cuba, and that the main American force was now almost 1,000 miles from its assigned station. Sampson started back for Cuba.

Unknown to Sampson, Cervera's force was first sighted that same morning, some 400 miles southeast of his own position, by an officer on the beach at Martinique. When word of this sighting reached Washington, some of the pressure was removed—the pressure, that is, that was keeping half of the Navy in readiness to save the Atlantic coast from attack. The Flying Squadron, under the command of Commodore Winfield S. Schley, was shifted to Key West, Florida. Schley was one of the officers over whom Sampson had been promoted. He now uncomfortably found himself under the direct command of an officer who had previously been his junior.

Word of the sighting was also sent to Admiral Sampson, and he diverted his force toward Key West, arriving on the same day as Commodore Schley and the Flying Squadron. They held an immediate conference: the Spanish had been sighted again, this time off the coast of Venezuela, where they were trying to get some coal. There were several obvious moves that Cervera could make: he could head for any of three major ports in Cuba (Havana, Santiago de Cuba, or Cienfuegos); he could go to San Juan; or he could remain at sea. Because of his apparent coal shortage, it was most likely that he would head for either Santiago de Cuba or Cienfuegos.

The Navy Department decided that Cervera would choose Cien-

[79]

fuegos. Sampson was directed to send a force to cover that harbor; he detached Schley, with one armored cruiser, three battleships, and some smaller ships for that duty. His orders to Schley were specific: that he "should establish a blockade at Cienfuegos with the least possible delay, and that it should be maintained as close as possible."

Schley left Key West on May 19. A few hours after his departure, the Navy Department at Washington received a report to the effect that Cervera had just entered the harbor at Santiago de Cuba. At first held suspect, this report was verified the next day; on the twenty-first, Sampson had received the news and dispatched a note to Schley advising him that the Spanish were "probably" at Santiago. "If you are satisfied that they are not at Cienfuegos," he wrote, "proceed with all despatch but cautiously to Santiago de Cuba and if the enemy is there, blockade him in port." Sampson made plans to move his own force to a point some 200 miles east of Havana, in the Bahamas Channel, to block any Spanish thrust in that direction. But he felt secure in the knowledge that by this time Schley and his "powerful" force would have neatly trapped Cervera at Santiago de Cuba.

But Schley was blockading Cienfuegos—that had been his assignment, and he was determined to carry it out. When Sampson's message had arrived on the twenty-third, Schley was still not "satisfied" that the enemy was not at Cienfuegos, although he had made no attempt to verify its presence. It would have been an easy matter to send a boat in to the beach with a scouting party, or to establish communications with insurgent forces known to be in the area—but Schley did neither. On the twenty-fourth, a ship arrived with a naval officer who knew the code signals which were arranged for use between the United States forces and the insurgents. He made contact and, when it was determined that the Spanish ships were not in the harbor, Schley finally started for Santiago de Cuba.

But Sampson's orders had advised him to proceed "cautiously"; and cautiously Schley proceeded, at a rate more appropriate to a Sunday outing than a vital military operation. He held his speed of advance down to a crawl in order not to outrun one of his ships, a converted yacht that could not make much headway against the fairly heavy seas. The yacht could have been left behind—it served no tactical purpose—but Schley later stated that he had not wanted to abandon it to the mercy of the enemy. Since the enemy was known to be ahead of him and there were no other naval forces around, this decision left Schley open to some criticism. Yet this was not the only poor decision that he made that week.

During the afternoon of May 26, Schley arrived at a point some 20 miles to the south of the entrance to Santiago de Cuba Harbor. Three scout ships, which had been in the vicinity for a few days, reported to him that they had seen nothing of the enemy. Schley then decided that there was no need to investigate further. It was his personal opinion that the Spanish were not at Santiago de Cuba and so, even though he was only about one hour's steaming from that harbor, he declined to move in for a closer look. Instead, he hoisted the signal, "Destination Key West via south side of Cuba and Yucatán Channel" (which would take him back past Cienfuegos). It was the commodore's intention to go to Key West in order to coal his ships—he had a collier with him, but the rough weather had limited the transfer of fuel.

The collier broke down soon after the squadron had left the vicinity of Santiago de Cuba, and efforts to repair her or take her in tow greatly impeded the progress toward Florida. The next morning, a scout arrived with more dispatches, including an imperative message from the Secretary of the Navy: "All Department's information indicates Spanish division is still at Santiago de Cuba. The Department looks to you to ascertain the facts, and that the enemy, if therein, does not leave without a decisive action."

Schley was not very impressed with this information, and was unaware that he was by now the center of all official interest in Washington. While Secretary Long and the President of the United States were anxiously awaiting some word from Schley, the commodore was carefully drafting the following message to his superiors in Washington:

Cannot remain off Santiago in present state of squadron on account of coal. Much to be regretted cannot obey orders of Department. Have striven earnestly: forced to proceed for coal to Key West by way of Yucatán Passage. Cannot ascertain anything positive respecting enemy.

He passed this dispatch to the scout, and continued on his slow westward journey. As of noon that day, the ships in the squadron had enough coal in their bunkers to have maintained a blockade off Santiago de Cuba for almost three weeks. In addition, there was enough coal on board the collier *Merrimac* to have filled all the bunkers on all the ships to capacity, with enough coal left over to have later furnished almost the same quantity.

Schley's message was received with consternation. Secretary Long replied to it by sending off a pointed order that "unless it is unsafe . . . Department wishes you to remain off Santiago." Sampson—who had received a copy of Schley's message—took immediate action, rounding up all available ships at Key West and setting out for Cuba. Meanwhile, back at sea, Schley had reconsidered his position. The weather seemed to be improving; perhaps he would be able to coal his ships after all. At almost exactly the same moment that the Secretary of the Navy was seriously considering having him court-martialed, Schley turned his ships around and headed back toward Santiago de Cuba. At about eight o'clock that evening (May 28), the blockade force arrived at Santiago de Cuba.

At daybreak the following morning, Commodore Schley at last took a look at the harbor toward which he had been directed some six days before. The first thing that he saw—just inside the entrance and in plain view—was the armored cruiser *Cristóbal Colón*. She had been in that position since May 25, the day before the American force had moved to within 20 miles of the harbor, and could have been observed at any time by even the most casual reconnaissance.

The *Colón* lay within easy gunshot, although she was under the protection of some fortifications guarding the harbor entrance. The commodore pondered this situation for a few days and finally decided that he ought to make at least an attempt at attack. On May 31 he led three of his ships in a series of quick passes on the entrance, firing at the cruiser as they went by. The Spanish answered the fire: no hits were scored by either side. The *Colón* moved deeper into the harbor the next morning, behind the shelter of some hills. A few hours after this, Admiral Sampson arrived and assumed command.

A plan was devised to take one of the auxiliary ships into the harbor entrance, and there sink her, broadside to. In theory, it was a brilliant plan, because if successful it would effectively trap all of Cervera's ships in the harbor and thus put them out of action—possibly for the rest of the war. It was also a dangerous plan, for the blockading ship would be exposed to point-blank fire from the shore batteries. Moreover, there was only one point in the channel where it was narrow enough for a ship to block it. A call went out for volunteers: hundreds of men from the ships of the fleet put in a bid to be part of the operation. The job was given to an assistant naval constructor (with the rank of lieutenant) and seven men.

Lieutenant Richmond Pearson Hobson was an unusual man, and a good choice for the mission. He had stood first in his class at the Naval Academy (1889), and was endowed with strong personal scruples. While in his plebe year at the Academy, he had broken an unwritten law by placing some fellow classmen on report for minor infractions of the written rules. The class decided that he should be severely disciplined, and so placed him in the Naval Academy equivalent of "coventry." For three years he was spoken to by no one, except in the line of duty; but at the beginning of his fourth year, when he was not only the academic leader of the class but had also been appointed batallion commander, a delegation of classmates came to him with a peace offering, which Hobson promptly refused. He had, he said, withstood three years of this foolishness. He could very well stand one more. In later years, Hobson was to become a member of Congress, where he championed naval legislation, and was also to be the first congressman to introduce a prohibition amendment to the Constitution.

[83]

However, in June of 1898, Hobson was busy becoming the second naval hero of the war. He and his men loaded a quantity of explosives aboard the *Merrimac*—the ship that had been chosen for the attempt—and, with a hearty wave to the rest of the fleet, headed the old ship toward her final resting place. Unfortunately, the Spanish fire was more accurate on this occasion than it had been during Schley's attack on the *Colón,* and the tiller ropes of the *Merrimac* were shot away. Without any directional control, the ship soon ran aground at some distance from the intended spot, and in no position to cause the Spanish ships any difficulty. Hobson and the seven volunteers were unhurt, and were taken into custody. The next morning, Admiral Cervera's chief of staff came out under a flag of truce to let Admiral Sampson know that the men were in good health.

When news of this daring exploit reached the United States, Hobson became the man of the hour. Congress rewarded his heroism by giving him the Medal of Honor and promoting him to naval constructor with the rank of captain. Eventually he was promoted to rear admiral on the retired list. (The ill-fated destroyer-minesweeper *Hobson* (DMS-26), sunk in 1952 following a collision with the aircraft carrier *Wasp* (CV-18), was named in his honor.)

While the Navy had been chasing around the Caribbean trying to locate Cervera, the Army had been moving ponderously ahead with plans to send an expeditionary force to liberate the Cubans. The first major movement, which was to be convoyed by the Navy, had originally been scheduled for May 16, but had to be canceled because Cervera was still at large. Secretary Long had properly advised the War Department that it would be "inexpedient to expose the Army or any part of it on the waters in the vicinity of Cuba" as long as the enemy ships were free to engage in offensive operations. It is doubtful, in any event, that the Army could have carried out the operation on time: it was having growing pains. Among other problems, when the President had issued his call for volunteers on April 23, the entire Quartermaster Corps of the Army had only 57 officers assigned, with sufficient clothing and material on hand to support the extant Regular Army of 28,000 men, and perhaps 10,000 additional men. Within one month, they were being called upon to provide food, uniforms, and equipment for an Army of 275,000 men.

But now, with the Spanish fleet definitely located, the plans for the expeditionary movement were rapidly pushed forward. The Army had a specific objective: Santiago de Cuba. It had been decided (by the Navy) that it would be suicidal to force the harbor from seaward, what with the shore batteries, the expected minefields, and Cervera's ships. Therefore, it seemed most proper that the Army should land troops a few miles up the beach and, moving inland, penetrate to the city from the rear, capturing both it and the enemy ships and possibly ending the war—with, of course, appropriate assistance from the Navy.

It was Admiral Sampson's firm belief that 10,000 troops could accomplish this mission in less than forty-eight hours, and he so advised Washington. Orders were issued to the Army—which, amidst monumental confusion, gathered up its supplies (they were scattered on various sidings throughout the state of Florida, mostly in unmarked railroad cars) and its troops, and began to load the ships. That is, they made a bold attempt to do so. The confusion was so great that any efforts to move the troops from their camps to the designated harbor seemed doomed to failure—until the commanding general hit upon the idea of spreading the word that the ships would sail in the morning: any troops wishing to sail with them had better be aboard. The actual method for doing so was left up to the individual units. Lieutenant Colonel Theodore Roosevelt and his men, just recently arrived on the Florida scene, commandeered a group of coal cars for transportation to the harbor and then boldly took over a ship to which three regiments had been assigned but which was only big enough to carry slightly more than one. Not to be outdone, the commanding officer of one of the displaced units, casually selected one of the ships waiting at anchor and sent a boarding party out to capture her for his use. The volunteer Army may have been

[85]

ill-equipped and poorly trained, but it lacked neither spirit nor ingenuity.

But, when the force was finally ready to set sail for Cuba, the orders for the movement were canceled. It happened that one of the Navy's converted yachts, out on patrol, had spotted what she took to be a Spanish armored cruiser and a destroyer—and it suddenly dawned on the military planners that, even though most of the U.S. Navy had been sitting off Santiago de Cuba for over a week, no one had made a move to determine if *all* of Cervera's ships were in fact in that harbor. The Navy was embarrassed, but once again advised that it could not permit the Army to put to sea until the location of all hostile ships was known. Some scouts were dispatched to track down the reported enemy force, and an officer from one of Sampson's ships was sent ashore to climb a hill, look down into the harbor, and count the ships. They were all present and accounted for.

While this verification was being made, the Army sweltered on the transports and the Navy continued its own operations. Reports of sightings of enemy ships kept some of the auxiliaries busy: on June 9, a converted yacht believed she sighted a squadron of eight or nine Spanish ships, one of which she believed to be a battleship. It was later discovered that this formidable group was actually five U.S. auxiliary ships. This squadron, in turn, thought that the converted yacht was a Spanish torpedo boat and had opened fire. But the distance was so great that the shots were not heard on the yacht, whose skipper thought that the muzzle flashes were a signal light being used in the squadron.

On June 10, the Navy and the Marines conducted the first landing operation of the war at a seaport called Guantánamo. It was a magnificent natural harbor some 45 miles to the east of Santiago de Cuba. The Marines landed without opposition, although Spanish troops counterattacked later. Four men were killed and some wounded, and a flurry of enthusiasm rippled through the American newspapers.

Partly as a result of the favorable publicity that the Navy kept

[86]

receiving—winning battles in the Philippines and doing all of the fighting thus far in the war—a rather hot feud developed between the Army and the Navy. The Navy needled the Army about its inability to assemble troops; the Army responded in kind about the Navy's inability to count ships—and when the Navy grabbed the spotlight by getting the first troops ashore, the rivalry became even more intense.

However, by June 14, the big expedition was at last on its way to Cuba. The Army units were crammed into thirty-two steamers of various sizes, many of which had been chartered for the operation and stayed under the command of their civilian masters, who remained responsible to their respective owners for the safety of the ships. Additionally, the working press had managed to mount its own expedition on its own boats, and there was more than one newspaper correspondent for every ten Army officers. The American armada arrived off Santiago on the twentieth of June.

Admiral William Sampson, the senior naval commander, and Major General William R. Shafter, the senior Army commander, went ashore together a few miles down the coast to meet with the local insurgent leader; unlike the situation in the Philippines, military operations for the relief of Cuba were expected to be conducted in cooperation with the local people. In conference, it was decided that the troops should land at Daiquirí, 18 miles east of Santiago de Cuba. Several diversionary moves were to be made by the insurgents and by the Navy, which would launch simultaneous shore bombardments at several logical landing spots along the coast.

It was originally intended that the Navy would have no part in the actual landings. When asked if Navy assistance was desired, the War Department had replied that the Army would do its own landing. However, when the time came to move the troops ashore, the Army discovered that it had neither enough boats nor sufficient experience for such an operation. So a Navy officer was assigned to direct the landings, and the Navy ships provided as many boats and crews as they could spare.

[87]

The transports assembled off Daiquirí early on the morning of June 22, and the troops began to fill the boats for the ship-to-shore movement. The loading took longer than anticipated, but by 9:40 the signal was given to the Navy to commence the bombardment. The shelling lasted for about half an hour, throwing up a lot of dirt and setting fire to a few wooden buildings. The officer-in-charge of the landings, impressed, later said that the bombardment was "heavy enough to drive out the whole Spanish army in Cuba, had it been there." Since the bulk of the transports had been concentrated offshore at that spot for almost four hours before any shelling began, there was little possibility that any part of the Spanish army could have been taken by surprise—either at Daiquirí or at any of the diversionary beaches.

As the bombardment was lifted, the landing began. There was no opposition: the only casualties were two troopers drowned while leaving their boats. But there was enough confusion to make up for the lack of enemy activity.

One problem was created by the merchant captains of the chartered transports: they refused to endanger their ships by bringing them in close to the rocky shore, not wanting to expose them to possible enemy fire. As a result, the Navy boats had to go well out to sea in order to take on any soldiers. The officer-in-charge of the landing, who was also commanding officer of the auxiliary cruiser *St. Louis,* took his ship to within a mile and a half of the beach in an unsuccessful attempt to give the reluctant captains some confidence. One transport, carrying 600 troops who were scheduled to lead the advance, hung so far back that it could not even be located.

There was also an evident lack of coordination within the Army staff. One group of ships which had been sent a few miles down the coast as part of the diversionary effort was promptly forgotten. Three days later, while someone at staff headquarters was trying to locate one of the division commanders who had apparently disappeared, it was suddenly remembered that he, his entire staff, and a brigade of troops were on those ships. They were recalled.

[88]

The double-turreted monitor Miantonomoh, *1874. This was one of a group of armored ships that was being modernized after the Civil War — a process that saw the passage of almost 30 years before any of the ships again put to sea.*

The protected cruiser Chicago leading the Squadron of Evolution which was composed of ships authorized in 1883 and 1885. These ships of the "New Navy" were considered to be fully modern, but each carried full sail rig. Left: Captain Alfred Thayer Mahan, USN, earned a distinguished reputation as a naval theorist, but was never free from sniping by his fellow officers. His last sea-going command was Chicago; the fitness report submitted by the squadron commander was so uncomplimentary that Mahan had to appeal to the Secretary of the Navy for an impartial evaluation. He was subsequently vindicated.

A major deficiency in the monitor-type ship was excessively low freeboard; the Terror, running with decks awash, seems ready to submerge. Below: Miantonomoh after reconstruction was finally completed. Compare freeboard with that of the second-class battleship Maine, next page.

The ill-fated Maine. *Note the off-centerline placement of the main battery turrets. Below: the brick "battleship"* Illinois, *an exhibit at the 1893 Columbian Exposition in Chicago.* Illinois, *built from the plans of the* Oregon *class, proved to be a highly popular attraction.*

The Oregon, *probably the best ship in the Navy during the Spanish-American War. Best known for her record-breaking run from San Francisco to Key West around Cape Horn,* Oregon *was also the only U.S. ship at the Battle of Santiago to have full boiler power available.*

The dynamite cruiser Vesuvius. In theory, an explosive charge was sent from one of the three firing tubes, propelled by compressed air, and an enemy ship would be damaged or destroyed by either a direct hit or the concussion of a near miss. In practice, Vesuvius made a good dispatch boat. Below: the armored ram Katahdin, another unique vessel. Katahdin's most practical service was as a gunnery target.

The protected cruiser Olympia, *Dewey's flagship at the Battle of Manila. The Flag Quarters are shown in an 1899 photograph. Note the amenities of an electric light, fan, and steward's call bell. Bottom: elaborate bow design of Olympia. This type of ornamentation had died out by the turn of the century.*

The Maine *arriving at Havana, Cuba for a "courtesy visit," January 25, 1898. Below: the* Maine *at Havana, Cuba, February 16, 1898.*

John D. Long (above left) was three times governor of Massachusetts before serving as Secretary of the Navy under Presidents McKinley and Roosevelt. A scholarly, conservative man, Long was a temperamental contrast to his one-time Assistant, the aggressive Mr. Roosevelt. T. R. prodded Long and McKinley to authorize military operations against Spanish forces in the Pacific by sending direct orders to Dewey. The coded text reads: "Dewey, Hong Kong. wasserreif pausatura Badanado Centennial titubandi loschbank Vovete offensando Caraquiez picarazado numeratura Spoilable appilante depugnere demidevil monosilabo atocharon tachonasen lienatte Crencha sparrwerk alienatote. Roosevelt." Translation is on page 47.

As a result of his victory at Manila, Dewey was accorded unprecedented honors. Special victory arch was constructed over New York's Fifth Avenue for home-coming parade; gifts (such as silver loving cup from the city of Savannah, Ga.) were showered upon him; and Congress created for him the new rank of Admiral of the Navy.

Similar honors were proposed for the commanders at Santiago — Commodore W. S. Schley (left), and Rear Admiral W. T. Sampson — but these were not forthcoming because of a bitter dispute that developed over two items: Schley's behavior before the battle, and whether or not Sampson's flagship New York (below) was too far away from the action for him to exercise command.

Two views of the Holland, *first submarine to be accepted by the Navy.*

Professor Langley's unsuccessful flying machine, October 7, 1903. Below: civilian pilot Eugene B. Ely demonstrated the practicality of naval aviation. He is shown here landing on a special platform on the Pennsylvania, January 18, 1911.

HMS Dreadnought, *the British battleship that forced a new standard on the navies of the world. Below: the first U.S. "dreadnought," the* Delaware, *commissioned 1910. Note the unusual under-the-bow gun mount, intended to provide protection against torpedo boats, but too often under water to be of much use. It was soon removed.*

The changing look of battleships. Cage masts replaced military masts on older ships, such as Kentucky (above and right), and Massachusetts (below, right) a sister ship of the Oregon, and were installed on all new construction.

After many errors, U.S. shipbuilders and designers began to turn out modern warships that were among the best in the world. Where earlier designs had been deficient in many areas — particularly ordnance — ships like the Mississippi (shown above in a 1918 photo, one year after commissioning) could stand up in comparison with any battleship afloat.

An old warrior which, in spite of problems in the original (1883) design, was still around to give service in World War I — the protected cruiser Chicago.

The most impressive contribution to the U.S. Navy's effort in World War I was that of the shipyards, both Navy and civilian. Mare Island Naval Shipyard met the June 1 launching goal on the destroyer Ward and set a new record.

Hog Island shipyard — a maze of building ways where once there had been only mud flats. In 1919, five ships were launched here in one day for another ship-building milestone. Below: view of the wet slips at the Fore River yard, where complete destroyers were constructed virtually under one massive roof. Raw material came in at one end of the building and ships were launched at the other, then moved back into the wet slips for finishing touches.

The transport Leviathan, *at one time the largest ship in the world, was a former German liner interned in the United States at the beginning of the European war and put into service when the United States entered the war. Leviathan carried almost 100,000 troops to France. Below: the pride of the splinter fleet, SC 131, after winning a homecoming race from Bermuda to New York in record transit of 56 hours and 56 minutes. August, 1919.*

The oil-burning destroyer McCall *taking on fuel from the* Maumee, *1917. Below: refuelling a coal-burner was always unpleasant, no matter what the weather but the crew of the* Leviathan *were almost able to muster a smile for the camera.*

Women were enlisted in the service to do yeoman work, "freeing a man to fight at sea." Elosie Fort and Lassie Kelly may have been the shortest and tallest of the Yeoman (F), but they apparently got their uniforms from a tailor who had only one size — and a pair of scissors.

Rear Admiral William S. Sims, wartime commander of U.S. naval forces in Europe, and Assistant Secretary of the Navy Franklin D. Roosevelt. The painting is "Return of the Mayflower," done in commemoration of the arrival in England of the first group of U.S. destroyers, May 4, 1917. Right: Secretary of the Navy Josephus Daniels.

By the end of the war, the U.S. Navy was overloaded with obsolete battleships. A Naval Disarmament Treaty in 1922 forced the Navy to scrap most of these ships, but left the way open for development of new weapons which had proved their worth in the war — the submarine and the aircraft carrier. Shown above: the final moments of the Michigan, commissioned 1910, scrapped 1925.

But one of the biggest headaches came from the newspapermen, all of whom wanted to be in the first boat ashore. General Shafter, expecting at any minute that hidden Spanish troops would open fire on the beaches, was not unreasonably concerned for the safety of the reporters and refused to let them ashore until he considered it prudent. Richard Harding Davis, covering the operation as part of the *Journal* contingent, was so annoyed that he went directly to the general. He did not consider himself an "ordinary reporter" and therefore subject to the whims of an arbitrary military commander. Rather, he styled himself as a "descriptive writer." ("Imaginative writer" might have been more accurate. Davis had been involved in the "search of the naked girl" incident.) General Shafter was not moved; he told Davis that he did not "care a damn" what he was, and directed him to keep out of the way. If the subsequent press coverage of General Shafter's role in the Cuban operations was not entirely complete or accurate, and if he is only remembered today for the fact that he weighed some 300 pounds, it is not difficult to understand why. Davis took his descriptive business elsewhere and attached himself as personal war correspondent to Theodore Roosevelt. Although Roosevelt actually played a very minor part in the campaign, he somehow emerged as the boldest military genius of the war.

By dusk about 6,000 men and some of their equipment had been landed, and the U.S. Army could claim a foothold on the island. The troops moved inland. On the next day, more troops were landed on the beach at Siboney, 8 miles nearer to Santiago de Cuba.

The Army moved slowly; it began to encounter surprising opposition from the Spaniards. Sampson had estimated that it would take forty-eight hours for the whole operation, but the ground forces took more than a week just to move to the outskirts of Santiago de Cuba. The time factor was to assume great importance—the longer the troops were in Cuba, the more likely they would be to contract the dreaded yellow fever or any other of a number of serious tropical diseases. And the longer the Navy's ships sat poised off the entrance of Santiago Harbor, the more likely they might be caught by the approaching hurricane season. General Shafter stood on a hill just outside of Santiago de Cuba, from where he could look down into the fortifications of the city; he considered the difficult opposition that his troops had encountered thus far, while moving through fairly open country; and he considered the slaughter that must occur should he try to storm this well-defended position. He decided that the only solution was for the Navy to force the harbor entrance, and capture the city from within. On the morning of July 2, he conveyed his thoughts to Admiral Sampson.

The Admiral flatly refused to enter the harbor until the channel had been cleared of mines. And he maintained that the channel could not be cleared of mines until the Army captured the Spanish shore batteries. There ensued an exchange of crisp messages between the two senior commanders, but the issue was not resolved. Because of the urgency of the matter, it was arranged that Sampson would go ashore in the morning for a personal consultation with the general.

July 3, 1898, was a Sunday. As Sampson, aboard his flagship the armored cruiser *New York*, withdrew from the ring of ships carefully positioned off the harbor entrance, the men on the other ships were putting on their white dress uniforms in preparation for divine services and the monthly ritual of the reading of the articles of war. Sampson and the *New York* moved smartly down the coast to Siboney, where the meeting was to take place. At 9:35, when the flagship was about seven miles from Santiago de Cuba, Admiral Sampson clearly heard the sounds of gunfire rolling down across the water.

The Spanish squadron was coming out of the harbor.

⚓

EIGHT

The Spanish-American War: Operations in the Atlantic, II

Don't cheer, boys, the poor devils are dying.
—Captain John Woodward Philip of the
Texas, passing the burning *Vizcaya,*
July 3, 1898

ADMIRAL CERVERA was disgusted—and not without reason. He had managed to steam across the Atlantic and through much of the Caribbean with a group of underequipped, undersupplied, and poorly maintained vessels without having sighted or been sighted by an American ship. He had stopped at several ports, hoping to replenish his steadily dwindling coal supply, but without success. He had pulled into the harbor at Santiago de Cuba on the chance that there would be an available store of coal, only to be disappointed once again. Moreover, once in the harbor, it became increasingly apparent that it would be folly to expose his ships at sea because a strong American force had moved into the area. He had waited too long to make the decision to leave, and found his small force trapped in the harbor by the decidedly superior American force poised at the harbor entrance like a hungry cat before a mousehole. Cervera did not enjoy being the mouse.

In fact, the Spanish Admiral had not wished to make the voyage at all, and had counseled against the stupidity of sending these ill-prepared ships over to do battle with the Americans. But the government of Spain, already humiliated by the refusal of the United States to accept her virtual surrender, had decided that if Spain were going to be forced into a war, even an impossible one, she would go down fighting. If there was to be defeat, it would be the defeat of a nation proud and valiant to the end.

Cervera and his ships had sailed over much the same route that Columbus had covered more than 400 years before, when he opened the Western Hemisphere to Spanish rule. They had come to this island which Columbus had discovered, and were now bottled up in the harbor of the city which had been the first Spanish capital of Cuba. It was an ironic and hopeless situation. To attempt an escape would be suicidal, and Cervera had put most of his crews ashore to assist the garrison in the defense of the city.

Then he received orders from his superiors in Madrid to try to escape, no matter what the risk; the nations of the world were watching his every move. He would either succeed—and draw the enemy naval force away from the besieged city—or fail, but at least the failure would be a glorious one. The Admiral urgently asked for the reconsideration of these orders. "The absolute and certain result will be the ruin of all the ships and the death of the greater part of their crews . . . I shall never be the one to decree the horrible and useless hecatomb which will be the only result of the sortie from here by main force, for I should consider myself responsible before God and history for the lives sacrificed on the altar of vanity, and not in the true defense of the country."

In answer, the orders were only reaffirmed: look for an opportunity to escape. If none should present itself, make an attempt when the fall of the city seemed imminent. One final plea from Cervera was also refused. The stage was set for the second Spanish naval disaster of the war.

And yet—despite the seemingly overwhelming odds and despite the hopelessness of the situation—Cervera might have succeeded. If he had made the attempt at night, he almost certainly could have run past the blockading squadron. But he was apprehensive about trying to maneuver his poorly manned ships in the tricky channel during darkness. Therefore, he determined that the escape must be made in daylight, or not at all. Cervera reassembled the crews of his ships and was finally ready. A last-minute decision—based upon the relative positions of the blockading ships at the moment of departure—called for the squadron to make a run toward the west as soon as the ships cleared the channel. With a full head of steam and all banners flying, the ships got underway.

The American ships were ranged in a loose semicircle with a radius of four to five miles, centered on the harbor entrance. Commodore Schley, on the armored cruiser *Brooklyn,* was at the western end; counterclockwise to the east were the four battleships *Texas, Iowa, Oregon* (recently arrived from the Pacific), and *Indiana.* Two converted yachts were close inshore at the western and eastern ends of the line. With Sampson and the *New York* off at Siboney, Commodore Schley as second in command of the force was theoretically in charge.

At 9:30 in the morning, a lookout on the *Iowa* spotted Cervera's flagship, the *Maria Teresa,* belching clouds of black smoke and charging down the channel followed by the rest of the Spanish squadron. The signal "enemy escaping" was hoisted, but by this time all the ships had sighted the Spaniards, and battle stations were hastily being manned. The American ships began to gather headway, converging on the harbor entrance; Commodore Schley ordered the signals "clear ship for action" and "close up" to be broken on the *Brooklyn;* and at 9:35, the *Maria Teresa* opened fire. Far down the coast, Sampson heard the rumble of gunfire and ordered the *New York* to head back to Santiago de Cuba at the fastest possible speed. He did not want to miss the battle of which he was supposed to be in command.

One by one the Spanish ships cleared the channel and headed west, and the American ships commenced firing. On the *Brooklyn,* closest to the enemy, it was suddenly realized that she was in danger

[93]

of being rammed by the leading ship. The *Brooklyn* turned hard starboard to avoid it, and in so doing almost collided with the *Texas*, which was forced to ring up emergency backing bells to keep clear. The *Brooklyn* continued around in a full circle, and then headed after the Spanish squadron. The *Texas*—having come to a dead stop—was effectively out of the action, although she tried to catch up with the fleeing ships and kept up a running fire as long as any were in range.

The other American ships took up the chase but were slow in getting started despite the eagerness of their crews to get into the fight. It would seem that because the ships were on blockade duty most of the commanding officers had not thought it necessary to keep all the boilers lit off and ready. Of the battleships, the *Oregon* was the only one that had kept full power always on hand. The *Iowa* had steam for 5 knots. The cruisers *Brooklyn* and *New York*, renowned for their speed, had only half-power available and were unable to come up to full power at any time during the battle because of a peculiarity in the design of their engines. For ordinary cruising, the forward engines of a pair on each shaft were uncoupled; to put them in use for high-speed cruising took fifteen or twenty minutes. On both ships, at the beginning of the action, the engines had been uncoupled.

Had the Spanish ships been in good condition, with clean bottoms and well-adjusted machinery, they could have easily run away from the lamentably unprepared Americans. But for most of the Spanish, the battle was quickly ended. Their impaired speed contributed to their defeat, but it was not the determining factor. The primary cause, pure and simple, was that the decks of the Spanish ships were made out of wood, some without even any iron plating underneath. The first hits from the American guns set them on fire; other hits severed water mains, and the Spanish ships were not equipped with secondary fire-fighting systems. Thus they were quickly turned into a squadron of blazing hulks as, one by one, they went out of action. The *Maria Teresa* was the first to go, and Cervera (who had assumed command when her captain had been badly wounded) ordered her

[94]

to be run aground as her own ammunition began to explode in the flames. In all, the *Maria Teresa* had gone about 6 miles from Santiago.

The last ship in line, and the one which had therefore received the brunt of the fire from the pursuing Americans, was the next to give up. She was beached a short distance from the flagship. A similar fate had befallen the two destroyers, which had cleared the channel just in time to get a burst of fire from the battleships going by the entrance. They were quickly finished off by one of the yachts (whose commanding officer, incidentally, had been the executive officer of the *Maine*). One of the destroyers ran aground; the other exploded and sank.

The *Vizcaya*, which at this point had suffered fewer hits than most other ships, had such a badly fouled bottom that she was soon overtaken. She continued on under heavy fire until almost noon before she, too, was put aground. To the *Vizcaya* went the distinction of causing the one American fatality of the entire action. A shell that would have been a near miss hit a sailor on the *Brooklyn*, killing him instantly. In general, the accuracy of the Spanish gunnery was nil; the ships were further handicapped by astonishingly bad ammunition: one gun on the *Vizcaya* had eight misfires in a row; another, seven consecutive misfires.

The *Cristóbal Colón*, a newer and more powerful ship than the others, had thus far escaped injury, and with the American ships in hot pursuit was running for her life. Behind her, leading the chase but not close enough to do any damage, was the *Brooklyn*. She was followed closely by the *Oregon*, which was nominally one of the slowest ships in the American force but because of her preparedness was right up at the front of the battle. Next came the *Texas*; then, well back, desperately trying to catch up, was the *New York*. The *Iowa*, too far behind, had dropped out of the race and turned to rescuing the crew of the *Vizcaya*. The *Indiana* had never been in the chase, since she was ordered to guard the harbor entrance. One Spanish ship had not yet appeared.

The race continued along the Cuban coast, each ship straining to gain another fraction of a yard. The *Colón* was holding her own and had a good chance to get away—but, shortly after noon, she ran out of good coal and was forced to open bunkers containing second-rate coal. Her boiler pressure dropped; her speed slackened. By one o'clock the *Oregon* had moved up far enough to try a shot with one of her 13-inch guns. It fell short; but a second shot passed over the *Colón*, and the battle ended as her captain gave up without any further resistance. Because of a poorly designed secondary battery and because the main battery had never been installed, the *Colón* was unable to direct any fire astern. At about 1:15, 48 miles from Santiago de Cuba, the cruiser was also run on the beach.

Thus ended the Battle of Santiago. The Spanish had lost 400 men; American casualties totaled one killed, one wounded.

At this point, Admiral Sampson reached the scene, having arrived too late to take any active part in the action. Now began the second Battle of Santiago—this one to be fought more bitterly and last much longer than the first. Who had been in command, and to whom should the laurels of the victory go—Admiral Sampson or Commodore Schley? Sampson, though removed from the immediate scene of action, had never been out of signal range of his forces; Schley, as senior officer present, had assumed command when the battle started. To Schley's credit, he did not at first try to claim the victory for himself. But, as time went on and Sampson refused to give him any recognition—not even mentioning him in the official report—his resentment toward Sampson, the man who had been his junior, flared into open and bitter public debate.

When Schley sent the following signal to the Admiral: "We have gained a great victory. Details will be communicated," Sampson set the tone at once by replying to Schley with a curt, "Report your casualties." The Admiral saved his rhetorical skill for this announcement which he sent off to Washington: "The fleet under my command offers the nation as a Fourth of July present the whole of Cervera's fleet. It attempted to escape at 9:30 this morning; at 2:00, the last ship—the *Cristóbal Colón*—had run ashore 75 miles west of Santiago and hauled down her colors." Actually Sampson had not even taken time to correctly evaluate the action: one Spanish ship, the *Reina Mercedes,* was still in the harbor (it would be sunk the next day while attempting to sink itself to block the channel); the *Colón* had surrendered at 1:15, and was only 48 miles from Santiago de Cuba. But the nation received Sampson's "Fourth of July present" with appropriate rejoicing, and President McKinley thoughtfully attributed the victory to "divine Providence."

General Shafter congratulated Admiral Sampson on the successful engagement and suggested that, now that the Spanish ships were out of the way, the Navy might reconsider his earlier request to enter the harbor and force the surrender of the city. But Sampson was no more eager than before to expose his ships to the dangers of shore batteries and minefields. The dispute flared anew; the commanders in the field were unable to resolve it and the matter was referred all the way up the line to the White House. The White House referred it back to the commanders in the field. The Secretary of War suggested that the Army take a couple of transports, arm them with bales of hay, and force the channel for the Navy. He also published the telegrams he had been receiving from General Shafter decrying the Navy's lack of cooperation, thus scoring a few points for the Army in the publicity game. Sampson, put on the defensive, could only make lame excuses: "I have been ready at any time during the past three weeks to silence works, to clear entrance of mines, and to enter harbor whenever the Army will do the part which the proper conduct of war assigns to it. To throw my ships to certain destruction upon minefields would be suicidal folly . . ."

The Spanish garrison resolved the dispute. It surrendered.

Admiral Sampson's disposition was not improved when it was later discovered that the vaunted harbor defenses of which he had been so concerned consisted of a total of eleven mines (not all of which could be exploded in a subsequent trial), four medium-caliber guns of fairly modern design, and an interesting collection of antique muzzle-loading cannons, one of which had been cast as early as 1668.

The actual capitulation took place on July 16, but the formal cere-monies were held the next morning. Whether by oversight or inten-tion, the Army neglected to notify Admiral Sampson of the time and place until it was too late for him either to attend in person or send a representative. The same petty spirit was to distinguish the occu-pation of the city. There were some Spanish merchant ships and one small gunboat in the harbor; the Navy claimed them (anticipating the receipt of prize monies for them) but the Army promptly occu-pied them and would not release them. One enterprising Navy lieu-tenant, sent to take custody of the gunboat, quickly evaluated the situation and blandly told the Army officer in charge that it had been properly arranged for the Navy to take the vessel. The ruse was soon discovered—but not before Lieutenant Marble and his men had man-aged to get the gunboat underway. The tug that was sent in hot pur-suit was no match in speed, and soon had to give up the chase.

Admiral Sampson tried to bargain with the Army; he offered them the harbor forts in exchange for the ships. "Although my forces have frequently engaged these forts and yours have not exchanged a shot with them, I await the arrival of a detachment of your troops to take possession, as they must eventually occupy them. I expect the same consideration." But there was no deal.

The Army finally turned the ships over to the Navy, upon direc-tion from higher authority. But it was to be a hollow triumph for the Navy—the Attorney General of the United States ruled that these ships were not subject to application of the prize laws.

The war—the one with the Spaniards, that is—went on for a few more weeks and was relatively uneventful. A convoy was formed to take a force to Puerto Rico, and it was handled about as efficiently as the Cuban affair. The commanding general of this operation, while en route from Cuba with part of his troops, changed his mind about the place of attack but neglected to notify another group of trans-ports which were en route direct from the United States. They got the word at the last possible moment—just before they attempted to land the unsupported troops against what could have been heated Spanish opposition.

[98]

Nor did the Navy make itself any more popular with the Army by accepting the surrender of a town that the Army was preparing to attack later in the day. The United States flag was cheerfully raised over the port office and city hall by Naval Cadet George Cabot Lodge, a son of Senator Lodge, while the Army units back in the hills were nervously awaiting the hour of the scheduled assault.

Needless to say, incidents such as this did little to allay the Army's suspicion that the Navy was trying to steal all of the glory. General Nelson A. Miles, who was in command at Puerto Rico, sent a "personal and confidential" cable to the Secretary of War in which he indicated his conviction that Admiral Sampson had given orders to the fleet to bombard the capital city of San Juan and demand its surrender before the Army could arrive on the scene. It was sometimes difficult to determine just who was fighting whom.

Peace negotiations began shortly after the fall of Santiago de Cuba, and by August 7 the Spanish had accepted all of the proposed terms of surrender. The actual surrender occurred on August 12. The Navy's role in the Atlantic was more or less finished; in the Philippines, American forces achieved peace with the Spanish, although the Filipinos, who wanted to govern the Islands themselves, were soon to cause problems.

As for the Army, it found another enemy. In Cuba and in Puerto Rico, the virulent tropical diseases began to take a heavy toll. Before they had run their course, they had killed about three times the number of troops that had died as a result of combat with the Spanish.

NINE
⚓

Aftermath

It has been a splendid little war; begun with the highest motives, carried on with magnificent intelligence and spirit, favored by that fortune which loves the brave.
—John Hay, United States ambassador at
London, 1898

THE WAR was over, and it had been a largely naval war. The victories at Manila and Santiago de Cuba were glorious and virtually bloodless; the entire loss to the Navy from enemy action (which included a few minor skirmishes) was eighteen dead—and one of those may have accidentally shot himself. As far as the public was concerned, the war had started with the Navy and had been won by the Navy. The Army, with its blunders too easily observed by the hordes of newspapermen who followed close at hand, was too frequently the object of ridicule. The Navy had refused to allow correspondents on the warships, and thereby gained two advantages: the movements of the fleet were conducted under somewhat better secrecy than the movements of the troops; and the many errors committed by the Navy went unseen and therefore unreported.

However, it was not so much that the American Navy had won the war as that the Spanish Navy had lost it. The enemy's approach throughout the conflict had been guided by a fatalistic expectation of defeat; it did not seem to occur to any of the senior Spanish commanders that they could possibly win a battle. Neither Admiral Montojo nor Admiral Cervera had taken the initiative—each, in fact, had carefully placed their forces in a position where they hardly could have avoided being destroyed.

But all this was not made apparent to the citizens of the victorious nation, who gloried in the superiority of its "new Navy." Great credit was given to the magnificent ships, to the dedicated "boys" who ran them, to the advance planning of the Navy Department—and to the fleet gunnery training that had placed the ships in such a high state of readiness for battle. "When our boys aimed at anything they could hardly help but hit it," wrote one enthusiast, "while the poor but brave Spaniards could hardly hit anything but the water."

This was patriotic, but not very accurate. If Spanish gunnery was pitiable, it was no more so than that of the American forces. At the Battle of Manila Bay, the recorded hits totaled 141, or one hit for every 50 shots fired. At Santiago de Cuba 170 guns were used in the action scoring 163 hits, or less than 1 hit per gun; and the number of shells fired from those guns is estimated at over 9,000. One ship alone—the *Oregon*—expended 1,775 rounds. And not one of the enemy cruisers had been damaged in any vital part of hull or machinery, nor had the armor belt in any ship been pierced. The Spanish ships had been put out of action by the fires, not the accuracy of gunfire.

But the war had been won and the nation saluted its heroes. In a wave of sentimental enthusiasm, the defeated enemy was included in the salute; a fund-raising campaign was even started to buy Admiral Cervera a house in Florida. (He was not interested. Cleared by the Supreme Naval and Military Court of Spain of any culpability in the defeat at Santiago, he was promoted to the rank of vice admiral and, later, became the Chief of Staff of the Spanish Navy.)

The first hero welcomed home was Colonel Theodore Roosevelt, the one Army officer who had enjoyed a consistently good press. His popularity was assured, and he was quickly boomed as candidate for the office of governor of New York. It was an election "Teddy" easily won. Two years later he was the candidate for vice president of the

United States, on the ticket for McKinley's second term—and was also elected. Several men had actually been considered for the second-place spot on the ticket; prominent among them was Secretary of the Navy John D. Long.

Richmond Pearson Hobson went to the Philippines to conduct salvage operations on the sunken Spanish ships, but he became ill and later returned to the United States. He was grandly received; it became the fashion of the day for young ladies to walk up to Hobson on the street and kiss him, and he became known as "the most kissed man in America." Such publicity did not hurt his subsequent political career.

Admiral Dewey remained in the Philippines for about a year, as his work there did not end with the signing of a peace agreement with Spain. (Since the Philippines had not actually been captured, only the city and environs of Manila, the United States therefore could only have a tenuous claim to right of possession, and the sum of $20,000,000 was paid to Spain in settlement for the Islands.) As for the Filipino insurgents, they had their own plans for the Philippines, and these were somewhat in conflict with those of the United States. Several other countries—notably Germany and Japan —were watching developments in the Islands with but lightly concealed interest. Indeed, it is quite likely that if the United States had not decided to assume control of the Philippines, one of these other nations would have moved in and done so.

The Filipinos had tried to cooperate with the Americans so that they might achieve their goal of self-government in a friendly and peaceful manner. But by February of 1899, they stopped trying to make their point diplomatically and launched a general campaign against American troops in the Islands. This marked the beginning of a little-known war that was to cost as much life and effort as the whole of the war with Spain, and was to last several years longer. Moreover, it was to be carried on without the overwhelming public support that had been so useful in the Spanish war. One letter of protest received by the Secretary of the Navy neatly pinpointed the issue: "What are we going to do with our Army and Navy in the Philippines? We are going to shoot and kill men who do not choose to submit to our authority, which they have never invoked or recognized."

American dreams of imperialism were little modified by such views, however. The United States was going to be a power in the Far East, and the Philippine Islands were going to be the main base of all operations—military, political, or commercial. At the same time, a new justification for such expansion came forth—the new manifest destiny. It was thought to be the duty and responsibility of the American people to help lead the underprivileged peoples of the world to bigger and better things. Some men of wealth and power and, perhaps, influence tried to dissuade the politicians from such pompous thoughts, but logic did not penetrate the vale of nationalistic glory. "It is a matter of congratulation," Andrew Carnegie later was to wryly observe to the Secretary of State, "that you seem to have about finished your work of civilizing the Filipinos. It is thought that about 8,000 of them have been completely civilized and sent to heaven."

When George Dewey came home in 1899, he was to receive honors such as never before had been bestowed upon any American. The parade up New York's Fifth Avenue through a specially constructed Victory Arch was without precedent; commemorative medals, loving cups, and other works of art came to him from all parts of the country. On October 4, the admiral was received at the White House by President McKinley. As a token of esteem, the East Room was temporarily designated as the Navy Department, and it was there that upon his return from the Philippines Dewey first reported to the Secretary of the Navy. The two men then went into the library where the President was waiting; next the admiral was presented to the assembled Cabinet. It was a gala, full-dress affair.

Congress voted Dewey a sword of honor—which was presented to him on the steps of the Capitol—and afforded him an even higher honor by creating a new naval rank especially for him: admiral of the Navy. It was intended that it should be comparable to the highest rank then in existence in any navy in the world; however, because of a clerical error, the actual wording of the act of Congress of March 2, 1899, made the title "admiral in the Navy," which was hardly as distinctive. The error was later noted, and corrected by another act of Congress in 1902. At that time, Dewey was nominated to and confirmed for the originally proposed rank. The acts provided that the incumbent would always be carried on active duty, and that the rank would cease to exist upon his death.

Dewey, Roosevelt, Hobson—each received honors, promotion, high office. Sampson and Schley were offered similar honors but the controversy between the two men had grown so bitter that it blocked any efforts that would tend to favor either of them. On the permanent Navy list, Schley outranked Sampson by two numbers; Sampson's promotion at the beginning of the war had been a temporary one. The first sign of real trouble came when a bill was introduced into the Congress to honor both men by making them permanent rear admirals. Sampson was to have an advancement of eight numbers on the regular list, Schley—who had been made a temporary rear admiral at the close of the war—was to be advanced six numbers. Thus, each would have the relative rank held during the war, with the prewar seniority reversed.

Friends of Schley raised a commotion. Their man, it was claimed, had won the Battle of Santiago. Why should his "reward" be to place him below a man who had nothing to do with the battle? Sampson's supporters not only took the opposite view—namely, that Sampson had been in command, even though a few miles away from the fighting—but suggested that Schley's behavior before the battle, when he failed to determine the location of the enemy and directly refused to carry out orders from the Navy Department, merited a court-martial. And thus the new battle was joined, with each man being championed by a sizable following.

The personalities of the two men had much to do with the nature of the controversy. Schley was a pleasant, gracious man who made friends easily and was a well-known public figure. Sampson was a cold, austere man who preferred to be left to himself. But he was generally considered to be a better naval officer; this is why he had been given the senior command, and this is why the Navy—and Navy officers—favored Sampson in the dispute. When a later bill to honor the men was introduced into the Congress—this one to revive the rank of vice admiral and appoint both Sampson and Schley to that rank—naval opinion held Schley to be unworthy of such recognition. The commanding officers of all eight of the ships that had fought the Battle of Santiago, including the commanding officer of Schley's own flagship, made a formal call upon President McKinley to present their individual and collective opinion against making Schley a vice admiral. Captain Mahan (who had been recalled from retirement to help advise the Secretary during the war) thought that such an appointment would be "a disgrace to the Navy."

Schley's support came from people who were more impressed with good manners than good seamanship, and from anti-Administration newspapers which intimated that he was being victimized by the Navy Department. Because of the dispute over the propriety of his pre-battle maneuvers, the Senate called for the Navy to produce the official record that it might make its own judgment. The record was so uncomplimentary to Schley that one newspaper charged, "The Navy Department has deliberately suppressed and falsified official documents in order to discredit Admiral Schley and advantage Admiral Sampson." Other newspapers attempted to set the "record" straight by giving their own versions, which clearly indicated that all of Schley's decisions had been correct; all his movements had been calculated to deceive the enemy. For example, one newspaper, ignoring the fact that Cervera's squadron had entered the harbor at Santiago de Cuba at about the same time that Schley was first getting underway from Key West, credited Schley with "most clever maneuvering" which "allowed the Spaniard to think that he had left [the vicinity of Santiago de Cuba] in disgust" so that the enemy "took the bait and ran into the harbor," there to be neatly trapped.

The controversy was not resolved; the partisans in the Senate effectively deadlocked any action to reward the two men. The Sampson supporters refused to give Schley what they considered to be undue credit, and the Schley faction refused to allow any bill to be written that did not give Schley at least equal—and preferably higher —recognition. In March 1901 Assistant Secretary of the Navy Frank W. Hackett, in a confidential memorandum, recommended that Secretary Long convene a special board, composed of three retired rear admirals, to consider the whole matter in open session so that the word would reach the public "in a manner dignified and orderly, that will carry a persuasive influence that . . . [the board is] developing the truth and nothing but the truth."

Sampson supporters had occasionally suggested that Schley must be "guilty" since he himself had never requested such an inquiry; Schley supporters finally persuaded their man that such a move could only be to his advantage. He entered a formal request.

The court of inquiry was convened on September 12, consisting of Admiral Dewey as president and two rear admirals. One of the junior members was challenged by Schley as being prejudiced, and was replaced by another rear admiral. The court was in session for over two months (with time out for the official period of mourning for President McKinley who, the victim of an assassin's bullet, had died on September 14), and recorded some 1,700 pages of testimony. Public interest in the proceedings was high, and newspaper coverage was heavy—but heavily partisan. Editors took every occasion to harass the Navy or the court, and did not hesitate in the use of personal ridicule of members or witnesses. The judge advocate, Captain Lemly, was cheerfully described by one Washington newspaper as "our fat friend" whose "façade is 'a thing of beauty' and his waddle 'a joy forever.'" When the court adjourned to deliberate on the evidence, the newspapers rushed to present their own findings. "Against the ugly background of the Navy Department's persecution of Admiral Schley" that worthy gentleman had won the day; his exoneration, in the eyes of the newspapermen, was complete. The newspapermen wore strange blinders on their eyes: young Captain

Hobson, giving a lecture in Cincinnati on his war experiences, was asked by a member of the audience for his opinion of who had won the Battle of Santiago. He replied, "The man behind the gun; or, perhaps, I might better say, with Admiral Schley, the girl behind the man behind the gun." The local newspaper ignored the pointed slur and made up a sensational paragraph quoting Hobson as saying "Schley did it."

The official verdict was not long in coming; it was by no means an exoneration. Schley was criticized for his "vacillation, dilatoriness, and lack of enterprise." His official reports on the difficulties he was having in coaling his squadron were characterized as "inaccurate and misleading." He was censured for making only a halfhearted attempt to engage the *Cristóbal Colón* as she sat in plain sight at the harbor entrance. The only comment in his favor was that his conduct during the Battle of Santiago was "self-possessed" and he exerted a "positive influence" on the officers and men around him. Admiral Dewey submitted a brief minority report in which he allowed that Schley had done a few things that did not merit criticism—but these were relatively unimportant items. Admiral Dewey was always very considerate for the feelings of his fellowmen, and his few comments helped to take some of the sting out of the findings. As president of the court, he also recommended that since the events under consideration were long past, no disciplinary action should be taken.

And there the matter should have rested. But it did not—the verdict was too unpopular. The newspapers heaped abuse upon the members of the court (sparing Admiral Dewey); Admiral Schley, who had, after all, requested the inquiry, now refused to accept its findings. He appealed directly to Theodore Roosevelt—now President—for a review of the matter.

Roosevelt approved the findings of the court and requested that the proceedings be considered as being closed once and for all. "There is no excuse whatever," he wrote to Admiral Schley, ". . . for any further agitation of this unhappy controversy. To keep it alive would merely do damage to the Navy and to the country."

And thus it was finally settled. Secretary of the Navy Long—who had been in office for five years—now submitted his resignation. He had remained with the Department through the last year or so only because he felt that the Schley-Sampson matter was unfinished business: and now that his former assistant had been elevated to the position of Commander in Chief he was finding it more difficult to to handle the routine business of the Navy. Roosevelt, as always, was full of ideas.

The Secretary and the President continued to enjoy cordial relations, but after Long's retirement they were to have a minor dispute of their own. The former Secretary set about writing a book on his experience in office, and a portion of the material, which was published as a magazine article in the spring of 1903, contained the following statement in reference to Roosevelt: "Just before the war he, as well as some naval officers, was anxious to send a squadron across the ocean to sink the ships and torpedo-boat destroyers of the Spanish fleet while we were yet at peace with Spain." The President took exception to this, since he felt it made him out as advocating an attack on the Spanish without a declaration of war. Long tried to persuade Roosevelt that his intention in writing the passage had been merely to illustrate his assistant's eagerness. Roosevelt acknowledged that he saw no malice in the passage, but maintained that it was awkwardly worded and open to misinterpretation. After several exchanges of correspondence, Long agreed to amend the statement in the book.

TEN

⚓

The Navy under Roosevelt

There is a homely adage which runs, 'Speak
softly and carry a big stick; you will go far.'
If the American nation will speak softly and
yet build and keep at a pitch of the highest
training a thoroughly efficient navy the
Monroe Doctrine will go far.
—Theodore Roosevelt, September 2, 1901

THE LITTLE WAR of 1898 had sharply focused public attention on the Navy, and in the flurry of enthusiasm Congress authorized enough big ships to make a whole new Navy. In May 1898 three battleships and twenty-nine smaller ships were voted, and four monitors—there were still many people in the Navy and the Congress who refused to believe that this type of craft should be allowed to become extinct, like the dinosaur it so much resembled. In March 1899 three more battleships, three armored cruisers, and a few other ships were authorized; the next session of Congress added a pair of battleships and three more armored cruisers. But by then the impetus supplied by the war had just about evaporated, and the succeeding session added no new ships to the Navy.

Thus, in a patriotic fervor, the legislators had climbed on the naval bandwagon—but with no more understanding of the need for, or the utility of, a navy than they had had in 1890. Through 1899 the appropriations for ships still specified "coastline" battleships but, at

[109]

the same time, required that these ships have "great radius of action." The United States had now acquired overseas holdings and responsibilities which clearly called for naval support, but the Congress failed to vote any significant sums of money for overseas support of the Navy. Mahan had made it clear that colonies and advanced naval bases were inseparable from one another but his message was lost on congressmen—they received their support in the parent country, not the colonies. The Navy wanted to develop the fine natural harbor at Subic Bay; members of Congress, however, thought it more prudent to develop installations closer to home, where the voting constituency could not only see them but be employed at them as well.

All this, of course, was good old American politics. In 1899, Congress authorized the construction of a $1,250,000 battleship drydock at the Portsmouth Naval Shipyard. When the dock was completed, someone discovered that another $1,000,000 would be needed to dredge the approach channel to a sufficient depth to allow a battleship to reach the dock; and it was late in 1908 before the first battleship went in. In 1901, a senator from South Carolina made an honest comment on a pending shipyard bill: "This bill is loaded down with expansion in every Navy yard. I am trying to get a little for Port Royal, because if you are going to steal, I want my share."

In the ten year period from 1899 to 1909, over $110,000,000 were spent on the shipyards in the eastern states alone, the real need for many of which was open to serious question. Five of these had no drydock which could hold the larger ships then under construction; two of the yards could not handle any battleships because of limited access channels; and three yards had docks that could not be reached by a battleship during low tide or if the ship was low in the water as a result of battle damage. (By comparison, the British navy—the largest in the world—was supported by six home navy yards, the largest of which had more drydocks than all eleven United States yards put together.) It was also clearly demonstrable that work done in the Navy yards was up to 50 per cent more costly, and took longer to complete, than work done in civilian yards. But military and fiscal considerations were of little importance when it came to dipping into the pork barrel.

Attempts were made to prod Congress into an awareness of the importance of the overseas outposts. The Secretary of the Navy pointed out that the Asiatic Squadron was 7,000 miles from the nearest United States shipyard, and that the ships had to depend upon yards in Japan and Hong Kong for repairs and support. He emphasized that the squadron was thus in an untenable position should any large-scale war break out in the Pacific—something that the growing aggressiveness of Japan made highly possible. Yet Congress refused to be prodded.

Taking one year as an example—1904—the two strategically important bases of Subic Bay and Guantánamo were given no appropriation; Hawaii got $18,000; San Juan was allotted $30,000. The same Congress handed Boston, Philadelphia, and Portsmouth over $1,000,000 each, and spread an average of $500,000 over the other continental yards, like so much political fertilizer. Congress had its own ideas about military strategy—the United States did not really need any overseas bases except as coaling stations and liberty ports for the ships. Any possible enemies were far separated from the United States by the wide oceans, and as long as the United States Navy could control the Caribbean area no enemy could establish any "overseas" base of its own for support of operations against the eastern seaboard. As for the vast distances in the Pacific, they were protection enough in themselves.

When Theodore Roosevelt entered the White House in 1901, the U.S. Navy ranked fifth among the navies of the world. Before he left office, it was second. His credo was given in his first annual message to Congress: "The American people must either build and maintain an adequate Navy, or else make up their minds definitely to accept a secondary position in international affairs, not merely in political but in commercial matters." He asked for steady shipbuilding programs; and insisted that the ships of the Navy be used in steady training exercises rather than "saved" for emergencies. "A battle-ship worn out in long training of officers and men is well paid for by the results, while, on the other hand, no matter in how excellent condition it is useless if the crew be not expert." ·

To back up this position, he called for the first large-scale naval maneuvers in the history of the United States. In 1902, all of the battleships were assembled in the Caribbean and placed under the immediate command of Admiral of the Navy Dewey. Further-more, when the exercises were completed, the ships were not sent back to their scattered distant stations but were organized into two strong fleets: eight armored ships in the Atlantic and three in the Pacific. Cruisers replaced the battleships on the overseas stations, and fleet maneuvers became an annual affair. It would have made more sense to put the bulk of the battle fleet in the Pacific where threats of aggression were very real indeed, rather than in the At-lantic where the British navy—by this time a firm ally—kept any potential aggressor at bay. But Roosevelt was apparently obsessed with the idea that Germany had secret designs on the Western Hemisphere—overlooking the political, strategic, and technical ob-stacles to any major expansion in this area—and so kept his naval strength in the Atlantic. The time was to come when his viewpoint would change.

Roosevelt's shipbuilding programs were given added support with the formation, in 1903, of the Navy League of the United States. This organization, patterned after a similar group in England, was made up of a heterogeneous collection of men with but one thing in common: an interest in promoting a strong Navy. Members included shipowners, ship builders, steel makers, exporters, munitions makers, patriots, and politicians—and they made a powerful and sometimes effective lobby. Their platform was that "Battleships are cheaper than battles."

President Roosevelt's shipbuilding programs were quite success-ful; the Navy was large and powerful enough by 1906 to satisfy al-most any ardent supporter. However, just as Roosevelt's influence with Congress began to decline—many of the legislators resented his heavy-handed tactics in pushing his pet bills through, and the naval building programs were expensive enough so that many congressmen had almost decided it was time to emphasize something else. Just at this point, most of the U.S. Navy suddenly became obsolete as a result of technological developments abroad, and Congress was faced with the prospect of having to completely replace the battle fleet.

It was a disheartening prospect. Until 1906, all capital ships in the world carried four large (11- to 13-inch) guns and a number of medium (8- to 9-inch) guns, mounted in pairs in independent turrets. But in December of that year, the British navy unveiled the *Dreadnought,* a powerful new battleship that forced a new standard of naval power on the world and gave her name to that standard. All medium-size guns were omitted, and the ship was armed with a main battery of ten 12-inch guns—giving it twice the offensive power at battle ranges of any other battleship then in existence. The *Dreadnought* also had heavier armor, greater speed, and more efficient machinery. It was also the first battleship to be equipped with turbine instead of piston engines. Other navies of the world, most notably the German, rushed to build their own dreadnoughts, and the U.S. Navy rapidly began to be outclassed.

The *Dreadnought* was not so much a startling departure from the norm as it was a logical step forward in the evolution of the battleship. But it was a giant step. The U.S. Navy had in some degree anticipated this development (having heard rumors about the British design), and there were two United States battleships under construction with eight 12-inch guns instead of the usual four. Another big ship had just been authorized, which would have ten 12-inch guns—the *Delaware.* But the *Dreadnought* was in service, and a whole fleet of sister ships were being pushed to completion in England and Germany. The *Delaware* had been authorized with the understanding that it would be the last addition to the fleet for some years to come. It had only been the year before that the President himself had declared that the Navy had reached sufficient size, and that future building requests would only envision replacement of worn-out ships.

But now, when T. R. went to Congress to ask for resumption of the steady and continuing building programs, his words were thrown back at him with glee by his opponents. It took all of his many powers of legislative persuasion to obtain new authorizations. One additional *Delaware* was voted in 1907; two larger ships were approved in 1908 (although the President had asked for four). This began the pattern which was followed for years—Congress cutting each Administration request in half. And it is possible that the President formed his recommendations accordingly.

In emphasizing the construction of battleships, Roosevelt was sacrificing all other types of ship. For at this time, the battleship was queen of the seas, the firm embodiment of sea power, and if T. R. ever had a choice among ship types he always took a battleship. As a result, other ships were only added haphazardly: three scout cruisers in 1904 (a new class of ship that later evolved into the light cruiser) and a total of twenty destroyers during Roosevelt's Administration. The only other type of significant addition to the Navy was the submarine—and this was in great part a gratis contribution by Congress. Although still in the experimental stage, twenty-seven of these little boats were authorized between 1902 and 1909. The submarine replaced the monitor in the affection of the congressmen because it had, to them, all of the fine advantages of that class of ship: cheap, warlike, and presumably of great importance in coast and harbor defense.

In fact, Congress was so interested in submarines that in 1901 it held special hearings on them. The Navy had at that time one submarine—the *Holland*—and another seven had been authorized; the Navy, looking around the world and noting that few other powers were building submarines, was not especially anxious to commit itself further. The Chief of the Bureau of Ordnance, Rear Admiral Charles O'Neil, testifying at the hearings, summed up the majority opinion:

The *Holland* boats are interesting novelties which appeal to the non-professional mind, which is apt to invest them with remarkable properties they do not possess, and to credit them with extraordinary offensive powers which have yet to be shown. In my opinion, they are ingeniously contrived craft of an eccentric character, which mark a step in the development of an interesting science but nothing more. Their so-called submarine qualities—which give them an attractive air of mystery—are of practically no value except for the purpose of temporary concealment for very brief periods, and the quality of submergence involves so many elaborate details and complications that it is a question whether the benefits arising therefrom compensate the objectionable and troublesome features it entails.

Still, he recommended completion of the boats then under contract, primarily to "find out what they are good for."

The minority opinion was voiced by Admiral Dewey. He thought that submarines were a promising development, and said that he would like to have had a few with him at Manila. He pointed out one benefit of the invention that other witnesses had overlooked: "The moral effect, to my mind, is infinitely superior to mines or torpedoes or anything of the kind. Those craft moving underwater would wear people out."

Navy experience with submarines had not been very encouraging —but this was in great part the Navy's own fault. When, in 1896, the Department had originally let out a contract for the construction of a prototype it declined to accept the advice and designs of the inventor and made a number of important changes which were to result in the boat being unfit for service. For one thing, the Navy insisted that the *Plunger* be equipped with a steam engine, rather than a gasoline engine, for surface propulsion—and it proved to be almost impossible to purge the boilers of steam and bank the fires for diving. A witness testifying at the hearings for the contractor, the Holland Boat Company, said: "They forced us to put steam in the *Plunger* against Mr. Holland's advice. When we built the *Plunger* and launched her and put the steam on, we found it was so hot we could not live in her." The company had decided to construct another boat of its own design, using its own funds, "so as to be relieved from the embarrassment of suggestions from officials of the government."

This independent building program was to produce the *Holland* which, in April 1900, became the first submarine to be accepted by the Navy. The government paid Holland $150,000 for the boat, although he had spent about $1,000,000 of his own money in perfecting the design. The *Holland* was the ninth submarine he had constructed. His efforts and interest, however, paid off—his company (later known as the Electric Boat Company) was to build the first nineteen United States submarines and an impressive percentage of all submarines built since.

The *Holland* was a gasoline-powered boat, slightly less than 54 feet in length and just over 10 feet in diameter. The 45-horsepower engine, in addition to providing motive power on the surface, turned a dual motor-generator that charged the storage batteries, which in turn ran the motor during submerged operations. It had no periscope (although that device had been used in the French and Spanish boats) and thus was completely blind while underwater. The *Holland* had one torpedo tube in the bow and carried a supply of three 18-inch Whitehead torpedoes; it was also originally armed with a rigidly mounted deck gun that could only be aimed by swinging the boat. The gun was later removed.

It is not too surprising that the Navy was unimpressed with this craft; but, then, the only navy in the world that was really excited about submarines was the French navy, which had launched an ambitious building program of more than sixty boats. Other naval powers were either at first opposed to the whole concept or just disinterested, but each eventually started building or buying submarines. Worldwide professional acceptance of the submarine as an important weapon, or even as a useful one, was a long time in coming: it was not until September 22, 1914, when one German submarine sank three British cruisers in a single engagement—surprising all the naval experts, German included—that the submarine finally came of age.

[116]

The best-known naval event of the Roosevelt era was the around-the-world cruise of the battle fleet, an event which was to serve many ends, but was originally conceived because of Japanese reaction to a flurry of open discrimination against the Oriental population in California. Since the days when they had been imported in large numbers to do coolie labor on the railroads, Orientals had always been treated as second-class citizens in the Far West. But this had never bothered many people, because there was no effective Oriental "voice" to speak for their welfare as a group. By October 1906, however, when the city of San Francisco forbade Oriental children to attend school with white children, the empire of Japan had become a strong and aggressive "voice" in world affairs. Japan had just beaten the Russian colossus in a devastatingly one-sided war and it suddenly occurred to the people of California, when they heard the distant rumblings of dissatisfaction with this insult to the Oriental race, that the Japanese empire might well explode in violent reaction.

Certain that the Japanese navy would suddenly appear offshore, the Californians were thrown into a panic, and this panic was fed by a number of newspapers and magazines that thrived on such sensational material. Roosevelt was urgently petitioned to send some battleships to the Pacific Coast to protect the citizens from the anticipated attack; but the President, remembering the dangerous position in which the Navy had been placed during the Spanish-American War by the self-centered demands of the cities of the east coast, was not now willing to bend to similar pressures. He answered the requests in his annual (1907) message as follows:

> We need always to remember that in time of war the Navy is not to be used to defend harbors and seacoast cities . . . the only efficient use for the Navy is for offense . . . In time of war there is sure to be demand under pressure of fright for the ships to be scattered so as to defend all kinds of ports. Under penalty of disaster this demand must be refused. The ships must be kept together and their objective made the enemy's fleet.

Having thus stated what he considered to be one of the most important of strategic principles, T. R. then hit upon a plan that would both satisfy the nervous Californians and at the same time impress the American public as a whole (and hopefully, too, Congress), thereby gaining support for his faltering naval building programs. He decided to send the entire battle fleet—sixteen ships—to California on a "training cruise," or so he announced. What he really planned to do was to send the fleet to Japan in a tangible show of force, and then have it continue on around the world—something that never before had been attempted by a steam-powered battle fleet.

When the Navy Department heard of this plan, it had some strong objections, one being that the ships and the men could never withstand such a grueling voyage. But Roosevelt overrode all objections, and the fleet sailed from Hampton Roads in December 1907. It was initially under the command of Rear Admiral Robley D. Evans (the "Fighting Bob" of the Valparaíso incident), but he was due for retirement shortly after the ships arrived in San Francisco, and another officer assumed command for the remainder of the trip.

It was an interesting and an exciting voyage. The ships covered 45,000 miles in 432 days, and were well received wherever they went. The Japanese proved to be especially hospitable and an immediate result of the trip was a noticeable improvement in Japanese-American relations. (A long-range result was not so favorable—Japan was spurred to a greater naval building program and the United States was thereafter to become, in all Japanese naval exercises, the standard "imaginary enemy.") And, as a training voyage, the results were superb. When the fleet once again sailed into Hampton Roads in February of 1909, it was not the collection of independent units it had been upon departure. Now, ships and men had been welded together into a strong fighting force. Thousands of hours of steaming in close tactical formations, of constantly being aware of the position of all ships in the fleet, of having to maintain machinery at a peak performance in order to be able to hold station had contributed to the change.

[118]

ELEVEN

⚓

Criticism and Reform

*I do not believe that anyone can understand
the Navy Department with less than two
years continuous application.*
—Secretary of the Navy Truman H.
Newberry, 1908

THE COORDINATION of the Navy's bureaus was almost nonexistent
during this period. The eight bureaus guarded their independence
with a fierceness that would have gladdened the heart of Patrick
Henry but was of little benefit to the Navy. Each bureau had its own
well-defined area of responsibility: the Bureau of Navigation, personnel and operations; the Bureau of Construction and Repair, hulls
and armor; the Bureau of Equipment, fittings and fuel supply; the
Bureau of Steam Engineering, design and manufacture of machinery; the Bureau of Ordnance, armament; and the Bureaus of Supplies
and Accounts, Medicine and Surgery, and Yards and Docks, the
areas their titles indicate.

Each bureau head was in command of a fully independent operation and was responsible only to the Secretary of the Navy, and the
heads of the bureaus liked it that way. Rear Admiral George W.
Melville, who had served as head of the Bureau of Steam Engineering for sixteen years, made a singular contribution to naval history
when he once stated that "the eight bureau chiefs were never called

together as a body to discuss anything; I can testify that my opinion was never asked on matters of navigation or strategy, and I certainly never offered any suggestions . . . it was not my work. I attended to my own duties and as a rule every other bureau chief attended to his, each keeping clear of the other's work." Incredibly, Melville was trying to justify the system, not make fun of it.

Since the Secretary of the Navy was too often merely a political appointee and unfamiliar with naval matters, the power of the bureau heads—each serving as the Secretary's "professional advisor" on all matters coming under his jurisdiction—was virtually complete. To obtain advice on matters of wider scope, the Secretary had to rely upon the device of using an *ad hoc* board—a board created for a special purpose or to make recommendations on a given subject and then disbanded. The Navy Policy Board of 1890 had been such a group, as was a Naval Strategy Board in the Spanish-American War on which Captain Mahan had served.

Some improvement was made in 1900 with the establishment of a permanent advisory group known as the General Board, under the presidency of the Admiral of the Navy. The General Board was charged with the formulation of general Navy policy, cooperating with the Army, advising the Secretary on various matters, and overseeing the work of the Naval War College, the Office of Naval Intelligence, and the Board of Inspection and Survey. But the General Board had no funds, no authority, and no franchise to interfere in internal naval matters. All other attempts—most notably by President Roosevelt—to bring about a reform in the organization of the Department failed. Congress enjoyed running the Navy too much to ever want the Navy to be strong enough to run itself.

Another serious problem was an acute shortage of personnel. Ships were being added to the Navy at a very satisfying rate—especially in the first few years after the war—but Congress refused to make any provisions for the manning of these ships. In 1900 the U.S. Navy had 23,453 officers and men and was reasonably able to carry out all missions and keep all ships in a good state of repair. But estimates showed that by 1906 an increase of 40,000 men would be needed to put all the new ships in commission; urgent requests to Congress produced scant reaction, and it was not until 1908—with still more ships added to the fleet—that its total manpower strength even reached 44,500. As a result, ships were dangerously undermanned. United States battleships had a complement of 17 officers, half the number assigned to the same type ship in England. To carry this comparison further, in 1907 the U.S. Navy was rated the second largest in the world and had 941 line officers; the British navy, which as always, ranked first, had over 4,000 officers; and the Japanese navy, which by this time had taken over fifth place, had twice as many officers as the U.S. Navy.

If Congress could be held responsible for the poor organization of the Navy Department and the low manning levels of the ships, the Navy itself had to take the blame for a number of no-less-important problems caused by a smug refusal to accept any criticism from within. Navy regulations forbade public criticism of the Navy by any officer, under threat of court-martial; and criticisms directed through proper channels were conveniently misfiled and forgotten. The Navy's own most ardent critic was to spend years in bucking this attitude and was only to prove successful by invoking, on numerous occasions, intervention by the President and/or the Congress of the United States. Such ungentlemanly behavior was to earn William S. Sims the lasting enmity of many of his fellow naval officers, and was often to place his career in jeopardy—but it brought results.

While still a lieutenant, assigned to the staff of the Commander in Chief of the Asiatic Fleet, Sims developed an interest in the quality of naval gunnery. For years it had been recognized that American gunnery was poor, but most of the men in the Navy accepted the low standards in the belief that this was the best that could be done. Sims heard rumors that the British ships on the China Station were obtaining what seemed to be phenomenal scores in gunnery practice, and he made arrangements to observe some of their shoots. He discovered that the rumors were true; and that the main reason for

[121]

the marked improvement was that the British had abandoned the traditional spot aim, and had evolved a technique of continuous aim whereby the target was kept in the gunner's sights no matter how much his own ship might pitch or roll. The British had also invented some equipment for use in training gun crews without actually firing the guns—most notably a device called a "dotter" which was similar to a penny-arcade electric-eye shooting gallery. The dotter allowed the gun crew to aim the gun and simulate firing, with visible evidence of the probable score that would have been obtained in actual practice.

Sims was highly enthusiastic over these new procedures, and sent off a detailed report to the Navy Department. The response was less than enthusiastic; in fact, it barely achieved a level of amused tolerance. Continuous aim, it would seem, was impossible. The Chief of the Bureau of Ordnance, Rear Admiral O'Neil (the same officer who thought submarines to be "interesting novelties"), worked out an impressive mathematical proof of this: it would take, he wrote, five men at the elevating gear of a 6-inch gun to produce sufficient power to overcome friction and the force of gravity in keeping the gun pointed at the target when the ship was rolling as little as five degrees.

Since Sims had personally witnessed continuous aim at work, he knew that there had to be some error in O'Neil's calculations. It took him a little time, but he finally discovered the mistake: the admiral had not allowed for the inertia that would be imparted to the gun barrel by the roll of the ship. As the side of the ship would rise, the barrel would at first tend to fall, and vice versa—tending, that is, to keep pointing at the correct elevation with very little muscle power required. Admiral O'Neil had worked out his figures using a gun mounted at the Washington Navy Yard—not on a ship. Sims sent back a triumphant rebuttal. It was ignored.

But Sims kept trying. By November of 1901, he had sent over eleven thousand pages of reports to Washington, which included detailed comparison of the gunnery records of American and British ships on the Asiatic Station. The British were averaging between 80 and 85 per cent hits, and were scoring them at the rate of four per minute. The United States ships were lucky when they made better than 10 per cent hits, and the rate of fire was not recorded. United States ships in other squadrons did not do even that well. Sims called the bureau's attention to the fact that at a "recent target practice by the North Atlantic Squadron . . . five ships fired for five minutes at a hulk only 2,800 yards distant, and only two hits were made."

There was no response from Washington. Continuous aim was impossible; the current methods had been worked out over centuries of practice and were not likely to be improved upon; American gunnery had won the battles of Manila Bay and Santiago de Cuba, and was therefore sufficient. Frustrated by this attitude, Sims proceeded to break all the rules and wrote a letter directly to President Roosevelt, challenging him to have the Atlantic Fleet conduct a demonstration. He suggested use of an anchored target 100 feet long and 60 feet high, at a range of 1,500 yards. Roosevelt passed the challenge to the Navy; and the Navy, glad to have an opportunity to show off its shooting to the President, and glad to be able to show up the troublesome Sims, accepted. All of the ships in the North Atlantic Squadron proudly steamed past the target, letting go in succession with every big gun on board. After they had finished, there were three holes in the target.

At this, the President is supposed to have said to the Navy: "Give him entire charge of target practice for eighteen months; do exactly as he says. If he doesn't accomplish something in that time, cut off his head and try somebody else." However, the statement was probably not quite so dramatic. Roosevelt sent a letter to Sims, calling him unduly pessimistic; but he did affirm that he was always happy to receive suggestions. And he asked the Navy Department to bring him Sim's reports.

Whatever the cause, Sims was ordered home and appointed Inspector of Target Practice. It may have been due to the direct intervention of the President, or it may have been the doing of several officers in the Department who were impressed with Sims's work and were in a position to bring about his appointment. Sims jumped into his new job with a will. He had dotters and a similar device, the Morris tube, installed in the fleet. He championed continuous aim. A routine of daily gun practice was instituted on all ships; and after three months, a progress-trial made off Pensacola shattered all previous gunnery records. The large guns scored from 40 to 75 per cent hits, and the smaller guns averaged 55 per cent. It was a fair start.

Sims requested that all gunsights be replaced with more efficient models. The old sights could not be adjusted to correct for wind or the speed of the ship or the target; the telescopes were low-powered, the cross wires were so coarse that they blocked out a battleship at 4,000 yards; and the sights were not shock-mounted, so the gunner was unable to keep his eye to the scope while firing. The Navy Department balked at this request, maintaining that it would take seven years to replace all of the sights. Sims thought it could be done in one. Roosevelt intervened and insisted that it be done, no matter how long it took. All of the sights were changed in about two years.

Further innovations included issuing a standard gunnery drill book and awarding prizes for excellence in gunnery—the best ship in each annual shoot was given a bronze plaque; and gunners were given from two to ten dollars a month extra pay (depending on the size of the gun) for making certain scores. Dummy breeches were installed and loading practice was conducted as an athletic event. The scoring system was changed to reflect the number of actual hits per gun per minute, rather than the number of "constructive" hits against an imaginary target estimated at the size of a battleship (using a small floating target as a point of aim). In September 1903, after a year of Sims's guidance, the 13-inch guns of the *Alabama* were being loaded and fired in 38 seconds, and averaging one hit per minute. The official time allowance for this size gun had formerly been six minutes per shot. In 1903, the overall fleet average was 40 per cent hits; by 1907 it was 77.6 per cent and improvement continued to be so great that by 1909 the percentage of misses was roughly what the percentage of hits had been in 1901.

Sims did not limit his efforts to gunnery reform. As early as 1895 he had been criticizing, through official channels, the quality of the ships the Navy was designing and building. Reactionary old salts in the Department who had been more or less forced to accept his suggestions on gunnery had been waiting for an opportunity to get even with him for his unpleasant ideas and his superior attitude. They saw their chance in early 1908 with the appearance of a highly critical magazine article entitled, "The Needs of Our Navy." Written by Harry Reuterdahl, a civilian, it contained too many of the same criticisms of shipbuilding that Sims had been making to be coincidental. The Department invoked the regulation against public criticism and demanded, in an official written request, that Sims report any part that he might have had in the preparation or publication of the article, and, additionally, that he point out any of the charges that he considered to be justified. Sims, at this time serving as Naval Aide to the President, was saved from a court-martial only by Roosevelt's order.

But the article produced such a storm of public controversy that a congressional hearing was called to air the charges. The hearings had actually been intended to put Sims, and a number of other officers who agreed with him, in their place; and to prove that the Navy was not deficient and that Sims was just a troublemaker. The members of the committee who conducted the hearings were at first openly antagonistic to Sims and his supporting witnesses, cutting short their testimony, and belittling their evidence, while allowing the Navy Department to give free and open rebuttal. But as the hearings progressed, the attitude of the investigators changed as they came to realize, in spite of themselves, the validity of many of the criticisms. The committee never issued any formal report of its findings, but the hearings nevertheless were a partial victory for the critics.

A partial victory, that is, in that the charges were in great part sub-stantiated and a great number of people were swayed to the cause of reform. But nothing was done to correct the single most important cause of the defects in the Navy's ships—namely, the complete inde-pendence of the bureaus. This lack of organization not only blocked cooperation in the design of ships but defects that appeared in con-struction were rarely corrected, because each bureau was unwilling to admit to ever making any mistakes.

These criticisms were directed at the fighting and defensive quali-ties of American battleships—qualities in which they were demon-strably inadequate. For example, the armor belts of the ships were not high enough above the water to provide sufficient waterline protection against shell fire when the ships were either heavily laden or filled with water taken aboard from battle damage. More-over, the belts did not extend far enough below the water to protect against torpedo attack when the ships were under light-load condi-tions. Admiral Evans, who commanded the first leg of the around-the-world cruise the year before, testified that when the battleship fleet reached Rio de Janeiro, with coal supplies nearly depleted, the side armor on most of the sixteen ships was nearly all out of the water. Other testimony brought out that when a heavily laden ship was traveling at high speed in calm water, the natural undulations of the bow wave along the hull resulted in amidships exposure of 3 to 4 feet of armor. A belt designed to extend 5 feet below the surface with the ship at anchor would not give much protection. It was also brought out in the hearings that American ships, once they had been launched and loaded, rarely ended up with the expected waterline—so that even armor that was theoretically well placed might, in practice, be of little use. And the freeboard of some ships was so low that waves would regularly break over the main deck in any kind of seaway, high enough to prevent employment of the main batteries.

These defects, it should be pointed out, were not entirely the fault of the Navy designers; Congress set the limits on the tonnage and cost of any given ship, and design was always a matter of compromise. To have given adequate armor protection, adequate storage capacity, adequate speed, adequate freeboard, and adequate firepower to many of the Navy's early battleships, displacement tonnage would have to have been doubled. And this is what was to happen in later ships as both Congress and the Navy became technologically more sophisticated in these matters. The ships designed in 1906 were twice the size of those designed in 1890; those of 1909 were larger again by 25 per cent. The designers were also confronted with other problems, because they were then working with weapons and systems radically different from earlier designs, using materials that had not been available long enough to prove their worth or reveal their weaknesses.

Some of the design faults, however, were plainly ludicrous and could not be blamed upon naval architects; they were the errors of line officers who considered themselves to be experts in matters of naval ordnance, although they had never fought in a battle. Some of the smaller guns they insisted on installing were too light to ever effectively repel the torpedo-boat attack against which they were expected to be used; many of the medium-caliber guns were so placed that only a few of them could direct fire ahead or astern—which, coupled with relative lack of armor protection in those areas, left the ships especially vulnerable. Main battery guns were sometimes arranged in rather strange fashion: the forward turret of the *Maine* was on the starboard side of the ship and could not effectively fire to port, and the after turret—on the port side—could not effectively fire to starboard. This was an obvious limitation, and was corrected in the next class of ships by placing the turrets on the centerline. But then another problem appeared—the 8-inch secondary battery of the *Oregon* class could not be fired within 20 degrees of the bow or stern, because the muzzle blast prevented the main battery crew from working their guns.

The brilliant solution to this problem was, in the next class of battleship, to mount the 8-inch turret on top of the 13-inch turret.

Both sets of guns necessarily moved on the same roller path and were trained by one set of controls and thus necessarily had to point in the same direction at all times. Yet, it was hardly likely that simultaneous targets for the two sizes of guns—which had quite different ranges—would ever appear in the same line of fire; but, for some reason, the men who designed this arrangement thought that they were "concentrating" the firepower of the ship. Also, one well placed enemy shell into the controls or the roller path would put all four guns out of action; and the machinery, which was electrically operated, was not backed up with a manual system.

The *Kentucky* and the *Kearsarge* were unusual in one other respect: the tertiary battery was placed with fourteen separate guns in one large compartment with just enough armor protection to nicely confine the blast of an exploding enemy shell, probably knocking out all of the gun crews.

The main batteries of some other ships could not be fired directly ahead or astern because the deck plating was so weak that it gave away under the muzzle blast. The forward deck of the *Missouri* buckled from a single shot of one 12-inch gun, which at the time was trained 22.5 degrees off the bow. (The solution offered for this by the Bureau of Construction and Repair was to restrict the arc of fire 50 degrees on each side of the bow and stern. The Bureau of Navigation, with uncommon good sense, asked that the decks be strengthened.)

But the most dangerous fault, and one that had been the center of a heated controversy for several years before it was again brought out in the hearings, was that the ammunition hoists of the battleships were so designed that there was nothing to prevent burning gases or debris from falling directly into the ammunition handling rooms beneath the turrets. Sims had called attention to this defect in 1901 in a report that later disappeared from the Navy Department files. "A baseball," he wrote, "tossed into one of the ports of the *Kentucky* class would fall directly into the 13-inch handling room, opening into

[128]

which there are 13-inch, and below which are some of the 8-inch, magazines."

In April 1904 five officers and twenty-five men were killed on the *Kentucky* when a flareback ignited a ready charge, and burning powder fell down the hoist into the handling room. The Navy Department blamed the accident upon the new gunnery standards that awarded scores based on rapidity of fire and recommended that the firing rate be reduced. When a similar mishap occurred on the *Massachusetts,* the Bureau of Construction and Repair blandly stated that there was nothing in the incident to substantiate criticism of the ammunition hoists.

The General Board suggested that the direct hoists ought to be replaced with broken hoists—in which the ammunition was brought up in several stages, each closed and independent of the others. The bureau justified the direct hoist by stating that the other navies in the world used the same arrangement, overlooking the fact that the British had been installing two-stage hoists since 1899. No action was taken on the suggestions. In 1906 an accident involving a direct hoist killed fifty men on the *Kearsarge;* public opinion was aroused, but even then it took the Navy another couple years to correct the situation.

The congressional hearings solved none of the specific defects in battleship construction; for, after all, the errors were all made in the past. Nor did the hearings provoke what was really needed—a thorough reorganization of the Navy Department. On this matter, however, Congress had not heard the last of William S. Sims.

Still, the hearings did have one immediate result—they almost got Sims thrown out of the Navy. Resentment toward him in the Department had reached new and impressive levels—and, as the hearings ended, with William Howard Taft about to assume the Presidency, it was determined that some "appropriate" action could soon be taken against Sims who would no longer be able to claim the protection of that office. However, Roosevelt got wind of the plot in time;

he sent for Sims's official record and was furious to discover that it was practically empty, containing no information about the many contributions that officer had made to the Navy. The President ordered that a complete report be prepared and attached to the record, and thus the plot was foiled.

In the process of making up that report, it was discovered that one of Sims's papers on gunnery had once been referred to the Bureau of Construction and Repair for comment; it had been filed and forgotten for three years and, when found, it had been half-eaten by cockroaches.

TWELVE

⚓

Men, Machines, and Miscellany

*"Is it true, Josephus, that you went up in
an airplane at Annapolis?"*
"It is."
"You are a fool to risk your life."
*"Albert, before you get out of your pres-
ent job you will be carrying the mail in
airplanes."*
*"Now I know that you are not only a fool,
but a damn fool."*
—Conversation between Postmaster General
Albert S. Burleson and Secretary of the
Navy Josephus Daniels, 1913.

A WORKING DAY in the Navy started with reveille at 5:00 A.M. and
ended with taps at 9:00 P.M. The hours in between were still filled
with traditional watches and duties, and the men were still primarily
occupied in keeping themselves and the ship clean and in loafing
whenever they could get away with it; but operating schedules after
the turn of the century were less casual than before. Greater emphasis was placed on training—on board ship, and in shore-based schools.
The industrial revolution and the Congress had combined to give
the Navy a fleet of highly complex modern warships, and it was up
to the Navy to keep them running.

And this became a major problem. The ships kept getting larger
and more complicated, filled with intricate and delicate machinery—

[131]

eighty steam engines of one sort or another on a small battleship—
and it became more and more difficult to find sufficient numbers of
trained personnel to operate them. The congressional personnel
limitations added to the problem, but they were not the only factors.
It was always possible to place an older ship "out of service," while
keeping it theoretically available for national emergency; and some
ships could be given to the recently formed state naval militia as
training ships. Actions such as these would free groups of enlisted
men for assignment to the newer ships joining the fleet, but would
not guarantee that enough of the men would be qualified in the
skills most needed.

The shore-based schools were one solution, for they at the least
provided a source of basically trained men. To induce men to go
into the critical engineering rates—and to keep them in the Navy
once they were trained—special pay scales were created that definitely favored engineering personnel. For example, enlisted pay
scales in 1905 ranged from $16 a month for an apprentice seaman to
a base of $70 a month for a chief petty officer, with a $5-a-month
bonus for the first, and $3 a month for each subsequent reenlistment.
Within this range, pay in the engineering rates was substantially
higher than in the deck rates: a first-class boilermaker was paid $25
a month more than a first-class boatswain's mate. (This may have
helped to relieve the personnel shortage but did little to reduce
the antagonism between the deck rates and the "black gang.")

There were other rates, as well as specific duty assignments, that
received extra pay—primarily because their duties involved increased
responsibility or overtime work. These included gunpointers, lamp-
lighters, signalmen, ship's tailors and tailor's helpers, messmen, drill
instructors (who came from many ratings and served at the shore-
based training centers), and the jobs of captain of the hold (in
charge of boatswain's stores) and jack of the dust (who assisted the
paymaster in issuing clothing and rations). Submarine men received
$5 per month extra, with an additional dollar for every day in which
their boat submerged.

In other moves to improve retention of experienced personnel, the prestige of the enlisted man was steadily increased and he was given more of an opportunity to improve his position. By 1905, legislation permitted twelve warrant officers a year to be given commissions—for the first time opening the way for an enlisted man to rise through the ranks to commissioned status. In 1913 a system of shipboard education was inaugurated, with voluntary classes in such subjects as reading, spelling, grammar, arithmetic and history. These classes proved so successful that Congress authorized the appointment of one hundred enlisted men per year to the United States Naval Academy.

Life aboard ship was steadily becoming more agreeable with the introduction of the many labor-saving devices made possible by the new technology. Electric potato peelers and electric dishwashers were a boon, and fit in nicely with the new "general mess" arrangement that had been pioneered in 1901 by a young paymaster. Under this system, all meals were prepared and served by the same group of cooks, rather than in the former isolated and uncoordinated messes located throughout the ship. The meals themselves were more varied, thanks to refrigeration and new techniques for preserving food. Bread, milk, eggs, jam, and an additional selection of meats and vegetables were added to the menu in the period 1902–08.

Telephones now augmented voice tubes as a means of communication from one part of the ship to another. The first sets had been experimentally installed on the *Philadelphia* in 1890 by the telephone company, at its own expense: one set between the bridge and the engine room, and one between the executive officer's stateroom and the general storeroom. The experiment was highly successful. Other communications devices included electrically operated annunciators between the bridge and engineering and battle stations, and various contrivances for signaling between ships—such as mechanical semaphore arms mounted on the mast, and arrangements for converting searchlights into dot-dash signal lights. And there was that incomprehensible but obviously useful invention, the wireless telegraph. Marconi himself had supervised introduction of his apparatus into the Navy. The *New York*, the *Massachusetts*, and the torpedo boat *Porter* were the first ships with permanent installations; and by the time of the around-the-world voyage in 1907, all battleships and 59 other ships were radio-equipped.

The change that perhaps had the greatest effect on the Navy—not only on living conditions but on operations as well—was the introduction of oil as fuel, replacing coal. Oil had a number of military advantages: it gave ships an extended steaming range for a given bulk of fuel, and it was easier to fit oil tanks into a ship's structure than it was to fit coal bunkers, which had to be accessible to the man with the shovel. Oil was more responsive to sudden demands for increased (or decreased) speed. It was cleaner. It required fewer men on watch in the fireroom. It was easier to feed into the fires than coal was.

The first American experiments with the use of oil as fuel for naval ships had been conducted in 1867, and sporadic trials had been made through the succeeding forty years. Oil was obviously a better fuel than coal, but certain strategic and economic considerations had prevented an early shift. Oil was not available in many parts of the world; and oil resources in the United States had not been sufficiently developed to guarantee a reasonable price for the fuel. However, by 1909, the objections had been in great degree overcome and the first oil-fired ships of the Navy began to appear. By 1910, all new destroyers and submarines were being constructed with oil-fired boilers, and larger oil-burning warships were soon to follow.

The Maritime Shipping Board followed the Navy lead and began promoting the use of oil: calculations showed that four oil-burning cargo ships could do the work of five coal burners. In order to ensure that an adequate supply of fuel oil would always be available to the Navy, certain lands in California and Wyoming were set aside as naval reserves and placed under the control of the Secretary of the Navy.

In 1922 the Senate was to launch an investigation of some highly irregular commercial leases granted in these reserves by Secretary of the Interior Albert B. Fall. Secretary of the Navy Edwin Denby—who was the first former enlisted man to hold the job, having served as a gunner's mate in the Spanish-American War and in the Marines in World War I, where he rose from private to major—had transferred control of the reserves to the Interior Department where, he said, they could be more efficiently administered. Within a few weeks, Fall had handed the first of several commercial leases to an oil company owned by a friend of his. The subsequent scandals were to rock Washington for years, and "Teapot Dome"—the geographical name of one of the reserves—was to become a household term. Fall and some of his oil-company partners were convicted in a series of court trials; the leases were characterized by the Supreme Court, in a ruling given in 1927, as "conceived in fraud and corruption." Secretary Denby was not directly involved in the deals and denied any guilt, but the inference of cooperation was strong and Denby was forced to resign in March 1924, "for the good of the party."

Programs designed to train and retain enlisted men—especially in the engineering fields—were not carried over into the officer corps. Where formerly all engineering officers had been specialists, personnel legislation in 1899 abolished the Engineer Corps and made most engineers line officers, and vice versa. At least, in theory. No organized program was established to give engineering indoctrination to line officers assigned to engineering duties until after a disastrous boiler explosion on the gunboat *Bennington* in 1905 had killed sixty-six men.

The chief engineer of the *Bennington* was an ensign who had never even stood a watch in an engine room prior to his assignment, but the Navy tried to hold him completely responsible for the accident. It was charged that his negligence had allowed the boiler safety valves to become so rusty that they would not function properly, and that this was the primary cause of the explosion. Defense counsel at the ensign's court-martial not only proved that the safeties could have had little to do with the event, but suggested in court that the real cause was the Navy's error in assigning such an inexperienced man to important engineering duties. The defense was able to prove to the satisfaction of the court that the explosion was the direct result of a problem within the boiler itself which a more experienced officer might have been able to prevent; the court found the ensign to be not guilty. The Navy Department was not satisfied with the verdict, as it was an implicit criticism of the Department's methods in detailing officers to duty, and returned the record to the court with pointed instructions to reconsider the findings. The court reconsidered, and "respectfully" adhered to the original verdict. After this incident, the Navy began to provide theoretical training in engineering practices for some line officers.

Another incident occurred in 1905 which could have had far-reaching implications, but was handled in such a fashion that it did not. This was an unrecorded mutiny aboard a Navy ship; unrecorded and therefore unpublicized, so that the rebellious spirit would not spread to other units. It involved a submarine—in the early days when submarines were regarded with awe and suspicion even by their daredevil crews—which was scheduled for a formal operational inspection. It would seem that shortly before the inspection, the commanding officer of the boat managed to get it stuck in the mud on the bottom for about half an hour. This did little to bolster the confidence of the crew, which was further shaken when he announced that he intended to break a few records for the entertainment of the inspection party.

The inspection commenced and the submarine got underway; the skipper gave the order to dive—and the crew refused. The skipper repeated the order; the crew again refused. The members of the inspection party—which included a future Commander in Chief of the U.S. Fleet, Ensign Arthur J. Hepburn—reasoned with the crew and tried to force compliance when reasoning failed, but also without success. The skipper was too reckless and submarines too dangerous. There was no dive.

All of the men rated a court-martial, but no courts were convened. It was determined that the publicity would be detrimental to the infant submarine program, and the less said about the matter in public, the better. The men were transferred, each to a different ship. And thus the matter was closed.

One of the legitimate functions of the peacetime Navy was in the exploration of the many unknown places of the world. The expeditions were small—a gunboat sent to chart the mouth of the Orinoco River in South America, or to take deep-sea soundings in the South Pacific—but they added significantly to the store of knowledge about the world. The least known, and therefore most fascinating, parts of the earth were the polar regions; and by the turn of the century, the most fascinating of spectator sports was the unofficial international race for the North Pole.

The U.S. Navy had always been involved in polar exploration to some degree, and had on several occasions sent ships into Arctic waters for surveying work, or to rescue the members of some hapless expedition lost in the frozen wastes. (Young Lieutenant Winfield S. Schley had commanded the operation that rescued the ill-fated Greely party in 1881.) But the Navy had never attacked the north country with the singleness of purpose that one of its members was to display: Naval Constructor Robert E. Peary, who was to achieve the disputed honor of being the first non-Eskimo to reach the North Pole. This became his one consuming desire: "The attainment of the North Pole is, in my opinion, our manifest privilege and duty," he was to write to the Secretary of the Navy. "Its attainment by another country would be in the light of a reproach and criticism."

Peary had become interested in explorations—in the general sense—during two official surveying expeditions to Nicaragua. Just why he first became interested in explorations in the Arctic is not clear, but it has been facetiously suggested that he was merely trying to cool off after tramping through the Central American jungles. Lieutenant Peary made his first trip north in 1891, while on leave of absence from the Navy; and it should be pointed out that even

[137]

though he was a member of the service, none of his many expeditions were conducted under the auspices of the Navy, with the exception of the final, and successful, push for the Pole.

From 1891 until sometime in 1908, Peary spent almost twice as much time on leave of absence as he did on active duty; the large costs of his undertakings were borne by various scientific societies, supplemented by income from public lectures. The Navy was not particularly happy with Lieutenant Peary, and the leaves of absence gradually became more and more difficult to obtain—requiring the intervention of a succession of Presidents of the United States, who could always be persuaded that the expeditions were in the national interest. Just before sailing on his last expedition, Peary's then-current leave of absence was canceled and he was assigned to the Coast and Geodetic Survey to make tidal observations in the Arctic. Theodore Roosevelt had arranged this, so that Peary's Navy pay could be continued during the expedition. At the time of this famous trip, Peary had achieved the rank of commander. He may not have put in much time doing naval constructing, but he had kept up with his profession, and had taken and passed the promotion exams then required of members of the Construction Corps.

Peary, with his traveling companions Matthew Henson and four Eskimos, finally reached the North Pole on April 6, 1909. The elated Peary hurried back to civilization, and sent off a batch of telegrams to announce his feat to the world: "Stars and Stripes nailed to the Pole," "I have the Pole," and, to President Taft who had assumed office only a few days before Peary had reached his objective, "Have honor to place North Pole at your disposal." Taft's bemused reply began: "Thanks for your generous offer. I do not know exactly what I could do with it . . ."

But Peary was soon to discover that the fruits of victory might already have been tasted by another man—a man who had accompanied Peary on his 1891 expedition and who had gone on to become an independent operator, Dr. Frederick A. Cook. It was Cook's claim that he had achieved the Pole on April 21, 1908, almost one year before Peary, and Cook's announcement of this—delayed reportedly because he had been forced to winter over in the Arctic—reached the public only a short time before Peary's. When Peary got this news, he sent off another batch of telegrams: "Cook has simply handed the public a goldbrick." And thus was launched a controversy that has never been completely settled—was Dr. Cook the first man to reach the Pole or was he simply a liar?

There was little doubt that Peary reached the Pole, as he was easily able to back up his claim with notebooks containing his day-to-day astronomical observations and other fairly conclusive proof. Cook, for some reason (he suggested many) was never able to produce his computations. But Cook had the jump on Peary in the public eye, and this was an advantage that proved difficult to overcome. And, much like the antagonists in the Schley-Sampson controversy, Cook was a warm, friendly man with a large popular following and Peary was a cold, strong-willed individual who refused to be bothered with anything as unproductive as "press relations."

The merits of Cook's arguments were few, and all rested upon faith in his veracity; tangible evidence was almost totally lacking. Since the great majority of the public liked Dr. Cook, he was believed; and Peary was villified as a bitter detractor, a vain egocentric man who was disappointed in achieving his one announced goal in life because "a better man got there first." The National Geographic Society appointed an investigative board comprised of distinguished and qualified men. After weighing all of the evidence and discounting the public relations efforts of Dr. Cook, the board declared in favor of Peary.

At about this same time, other evidence began to weigh against Cook's veracity: an earlier claim to have been the first man to climb Mt. McKinley, at 20,300 feet the highest peak in North America, came under a heavy shadow of doubt when the guides who had accompanied him on the climb (which, among other honors, had won for him presidency of the Explorers Club) stated that he had not actually climbed the mountain, but only a spur. Two other men publicly stated that they had been offered $4,000 by Dr. Cook to fabricate mathematical data to substantiate the North Pole claim. Statements made by Cook were discredited. (For instance, it was determined that his food supply, as published in a "first person" account in a New York newspaper, would at best be adequate to sustain life for only half the time he had supposedly been out on the ice.)

It would now seem that Dr. Cook was indeed, as the New York *Times* called him in 1910, "the King of the Thimbleriggers." He quickly fell into disgrace, and dropped into a pathetic obscurity which was destined to be broken only by further disgrace. Cook went into vaudeville, sandwiched on the bill between "a mimic and an acrobat," as his press notices read, "which is quite a fitting place on the program, and he is telling audiences nightly how he discovered the North Pole." He was later tried and convicted of mail fraud in connection with a Texas oil company—and, despite his pleas that he had been an innocent dupe, was sent to prison. He suffered a stroke in 1940 and was given a full pardon by President Franklin D. Roosevelt. He died a few months later. In 1955 and 1956, a party headed by the director of the Boston Museum of Science located the apparent "summit of Mt. McKinley" from which Dr. Cook had taken a group of photographs. It was 19.5 miles from the true summit, altitude 5,300 feet.

Peary, having achieved the major goal of his life, returned to an active Navy career. He received a regular promotion to the rank of captain in 1910, and a congressional promotion to "civil engineer with the rank of rear admiral" to date from April 6, 1909—the date of his success. The congressional action was by no means unanimous— Dr. Cook had many supporters in Congress, and it looked, for a time, as if another Schley-Sampson deadlock might occur. Peary devoted the remaining ten years of his life to promoting the cause of a new and intriguing science: aviation.

This was a science destined within a few short years to bring about radical change in naval and military operations.

The Navy had first taken a cautious look at efforts being made to send man into the sky with the freedom of the birds in March 1898, when Assistant Secretary Roosevelt officially took notice of the experiments of Professor Samuel Langley. T. R. sent a memorandum to the Secretary: "It seems to me worthwhile for this government to try whether it will not work on a large enough scale to be of use in the event of war," and recommended that two officers "of scientific attainments and practical ability" be appointed to a joint Army-Navy board to investigate the device that Langley had constructed.

The Navy members of the board turned in a favorable report; however, the Bureau of Construction shared neither the opinion of the board nor the enthusiasm of Mr. Roosevelt. The airplane, it announced, "pertains strictly to the land service and not the Navy." The Army supported the experiments for several years, but Langley's efforts to carry man aloft in a power-driven machine proved unsuccessful, and the Army, too, lost interest.

The Wright Brothers found a place in history in 1903 when they succeeded where Langley had failed, and theory became proven fact. Man could fly, even if only for a few seconds. By 1908 development of the flying machine had progressed to a point where the Army was once again interested, and the Wrights staged a demonstration at Fort Myer, Virginia. A Navy officer was present as a representative of the Department, and was scheduled to be a passenger on one of the flights. But an Army officer who happened to be present, asked Lieutenant George Sweet if he might take his place. Thus, Lieutenant Thomas E. Selfridge was fated to become the first military casualty of aviation. Sweet was a large and heavy man, and Orville Wright had installed oversize propellers on the plane to compensate for his weight. One of the propellers clipped a rudder brace while in flight, and the plane crashed. Lieutenant Selfridge died a few hours later.

In spite of this tragic accident, the Army was impressed and ordered an airplane to be constructed for its use. Lieutenant Sweet was also impressed, but was unable to convince the Navy Department of the value of the invention. The Army obtained delivery of its first plane on August 1909. As for the Navy, it adopted an attitude of cautious watchfulness; all recommendations for the purchase of an airplane were "deferred."

Notwithstanding these events, public interest in aviation grew rapidly, and by 1910 the Navy Department was receiving so many inquiries, suggestions, and solicitations from civilian enthusiasts that an officer was assigned specifically to handle them. Captain W. I. Chambers may not himself have been completely convinced of the virtues of airplanes when he took over the "aviation desk," but it was not long before the enthusiasm of interested civilians began to have an influence on him. He decided to do something to encourage active Navy support of aviation, something which would demonstrate the potential of naval aviation at the same time.

Chambers had heard that a German merchant shipping line was preparing a vessel able to launch airplanes (the shipping line involved thought that this could be a good way to speed up their mail service and thus gain a competitive edge in transocean contracts). Chambers, however, determined that the U.S. Navy should have the honor of first flying an airplane from a ship, and obtained permission to have a suitable wooden platform installed on the cruiser *Birmingham*. The Navy, of course, had neither plane nor pilots, so Captain Chambers enlisted the aid of a civilian, Eugene Ely, who was an employee of airplane builder Glenn H. Curtiss. (Chambers had first approached the Wrights, but they declined.)

On November 14, 1910, with the *Birmingham* sitting in Hampton Roads, Ely and his plane took off from the platform and flew over to the beach for a landing. It was a poor day for such a historic event: intermittent rain and hail showers cut visibility sharply. The event almost ended before it really began. The plane dipped so low toward the water after takeoff that it touched the water, and spray seriously hampered Ely's vision. But the demonstration was a success, and naval interest in aviation was increased. Ely's employer offered to train a Navy officer, at his own expense, to be a pilot. The offer was accepted.

In a follow-up demonstration on the West Coast, on January 18, 1911, Ely both landed on and took off from the armored cruiser *Pennsylvania* while she was anchored in San Francisco Bay. Experience had prompted Ely to be more cautious: on this trip, he wore a bicycle tire inner tube around his waist as a life preserver.

One week later, Glenn Curtiss successfully demonstrated an airplane designed to be operated from the surface of the water; and with this event, attention had been sufficiently aroused in the potential of naval aviation that Congress was moved to appropriate the sum of $25,000 for this use. The Navy ordered its first airplane, a 45-mile-an-hour seaplane appropriately designated the A-1; and a few weeks later, in April, the Navy got its first pilot. Lieutenant Theodore G. Ellyson, having satisfactorily completed his course of instruction with Curtiss, was designated Navy Air Pilot #1. (The official title was changed to Naval Aviator in 1915).

Two more fledgling aviators were sent to the civilian experts for training—one to the Wrights and one to Curtiss. Then there were three; and they themselves trained the fourth. An aviation camp was established at Annapolis in August 1911; more planes and more pilots were added, and the Marine Corps entered the world of aviation early in 1912. Technological progress kept pace—in 1912 the catapult was perfected and a plane was successfully launched therefrom; and radio transmissions were made from an airplane to a ship.

The following year saw the first naval aviation fatality when Ensign William D. Billingsley was thrown from his plane in turbulent air and fell 1,600 feet to his death. Lieutenant John H. Towers, riding as a passenger, was also thrown from his seat but managed to hold on to a strut as the pilotless airplane crashed. He was seriously injured, but recovered. As a result of this accident, seat belts became mandatory equipment for all pilots and passengers.

And in 1914, naval aviation received its baptism of fire. This was at Veracruz, Mexico, while several airplanes were being employed in reconnaissance missions. Veracruz was but one of the various campaigns in which the Navy was engaged in the years before World

War I—campaigns in China, the Philippines, Haiti, Nicaragua—but is most notable for two reasons: the first use of naval aviation in combat, and for bringing about the revival of the rank of vice admiral.

In April 1914, a Navy paymaster and two enlisted men from the dispatch-boat *Dolphin* were arrested at Tampico, Mexico, apparently as a show of political strength by a government that had not been formally recognized by the United States. The arrest was quickly canceled, however, and an informal apology was sent to the American commander in the area, Rear Admiral Henry T. Mayo. But Admiral Mayo, feeling that "American rights" were at stake, demanded a formal apology, punishment for the man responsible for the arrest, and a national salute of twenty-one guns.

The apology was given, but punishment of the arresting officer was not forthcoming and the national salute was not fired. The United States government stepped in, as Secretary of State William Jennings Bryan delivered an ultimatum to the Mexican government, backing up Admiral Mayo's demands. President Woodrow Wilson sent a strongly worded note. The situation rapidly deteriorated; Wilson went before Congress to obtain approval for the use of American naval and military forces as necessary to force proper respect from the Mexican government. Marines were landed at Veracruz, and there were a number of skirmishes with Mexican troops and Mexican naval cadets. Two aviation detachments were ordered to join the fleet, with a total of five airplanes, four pilots, and three student pilots. One of the detachments, under the command of Lieutenant Junior Grade P. L. N. Bellinger, conducted scouting missions on forty-three different days, and on one of them was fired upon by the Mexicans; the other detachment was in an area where there was no action, and conducted routine training flights. A change in government at Mexico City eventually settled the diplomatic crisis.

But another international matter grew out of the Veracruz incident. The Secretary of State committed something of a blunder by requesting—through the American ambassador at London—that the

British government order the senior British naval commander in the Veracruz area, Rear Admiral Sir Christopher Craddock, to place himself under the command of a less senior American officer, Rear Admiral Mayo. The British responded with alacrity, by telling Admiral Craddock to clear out and leave the American in control if things got hot in his vicinity. This incident had little effect upon military operations at Veracruz, but did serve to open the eyes of a number of congressmen to the facts of military life on overseas stations—seniority per se carries with it certain advantages in diplomatic relations with the services of other nations, and the United States had, for too many years, been placing its commanders in necessarily subordinate positions because there were no provisions for any naval officer to hold comparatively high ranks. The earlier wrangling over the bills to appoint Schley and Sampson to the rank of vice admiral had served to block the possibility of anyone else achieving that rank; but now, with both of those officers deceased, the way was clear to revive the rank, and this was speedily done. Fleet commanders in chief were appointed vice admiral, which placed them on a reasonable par with their foreign counterparts.

It was the first time that the Navy had any officers senior to rear admiral, with the exception of Admiral of the Navy Dewey, since the last of the Civil War vice admirals had retired and Admiral David Dixon Porter (who held the honorific office of "Admiral of the Navy" as the only admiral in the Navy—a post not to be confused with Dewey's higher rank) had died.

One American naval officer had the opportunity, during these interim years, to become an admiral—but not in his own navy. In 1900, the *Kentucky*, en route through the Mediterranean to duty on the Asiatic Station, stopped off in Turkey to collect $90,000 as indemnity for American property damaged during a recent disturbance in that country. Four officers from the ship journeyed to Constantinople where they were royally received by the Sultan of Turkey himself at a banquet in their honor. The food was served on gold plates, and entertainment was provided by an orchestra composed of sixteen of the Sultan's sons. When the dinner was finished, the Americans were invited into the ruler's private apartments, where the Sultan exhibited a keen interest in the U.S. Navy. It would seem that Turkey had just purchased a cruiser, which had been built in Philadelphia, and the Sultan was looking for an American naval officer to take command of the ship—and the rest of the Turkish navy as well. He was impressed by one of the four Americans present at his dinner; and thus was Lieutenant William A. Moffett, ten years out of the Naval Academy, offered the post of Admiral of the Turkish navy. Lieutenant Moffett declined.

⚓

THIRTEEN

Neutrality and Preparedness

> *October 29 . . . I was* amazed *yesterday to*
> *get an official letter signed by Chief Bureau*
> *Navigation, saying that (showing certain fig-*
> *ures) we could cut down the crews of certain*
> *vessels and stations, and have more men in*
> *the Navy than are needed! . . .*
>
> From the diary of Rear Admiral Bradley
> A. Fiske, Aide for Operations, 1914

WHEREAS the Administrations of McKinley and Roosevelt (1897–1908) had moved more and more into the international arena, the policies of President William H. Taft eschewed active involvement in foreign disputes. However, Taft was not blind to the realities of world politics and, while maintaining an outward attitude of "absolute neutrality" he hedged his bets somewhat by attempting to continue the naval programs of his predecessors. A growing Anglo-German race for naval supremacy prompted the President to seek a position for the U.S. Navy that was somewhere in between the two European giants, and also gave him a convenient justification for his program—the threat of an attack by the ever present German bogeyman. This was borrowed from Roosevelt, but the threat was no more valid than it had been previously; however, it could be relied upon to influence some members of Congress.

The two real reasons why Taft wished to continue expanding the already powerful fleet were not so politically acceptable. The first was to maintain sufficient naval power in relation to the European navies so that the United States would continue to be a force with which to be reckoned, whether backing up her pretensions to neutrality or in actively influencing the outcome of any future struggle between England and Germany. The second was an unannounced determination to enter more fully into the political and commercial activities of the Orient—a determination that needed the support of tangible military force. The previous Administration had asserted that all nations should have an equal right and opportunity (the so-called "Open Door" policy) to participate in Far Eastern trade, especially with regard to China. That massive but disorganized country had been "invaded" by several European powers, each of which established strong colonies and controlled the commerce of a large portion. There was, however, a wide difference between "assertions" and active participation in Chinese affairs; a difference that could, in great part, be resolved by the presence of a strong Pacific fleet.

And so the Taft Administration sought continued shipbuilding appropriations. The program was supported by the recommendations of the General Board, and editorial opinion throughout the country was in substantial agreement that the Navy should be kept superior to that of Germany. This consensus, however, did not—as usual—have much effect upon any naval programs as voted by Congress. One or two battleships a year were authorized, and in the compromise moves necessary to get even this token support the Administration continued to sacrifice any hopes for the building of a balanced fleet. The battleship was the symbol of naval power, and the importance of ships that would be needed to support the battle fleet—the cruisers, the antisubmarine and antitorpedo-boat ships, and the auxiliary ships—were downgraded just as they had been under Roosevelt.

It should not be inferred that the Congress had lost interest in the Navy; that the legislators had turned their fiscal attention to other programs which needed emphasis. On the contrary, the Navy had never been so popular, and during the Taft Administration naval appropriations reached an all-time high. Congress felt that shipyards, for example, were more important than ships.

The shipyard cult may also be credited with preventing one of the more sensible strategic moves that had been proposed in many years. The Administration made an attempt to transfer the battle fleet from the Atlantic, where it faced no real enemies (and even the Administration was willing to admit this) to the Pacific, where the policies in regard to China and Japan could at any time result in serious problems. However logical this move may have been, Congress balked because, as Secretary of the Navy George von Lengerke Meyer caustically observed, moving the fleet to the Pacific would have automatically put "most of the Navy yards on the east coast out of business." Thus the ships remained in the Atlantic. The only concession to the needs of the Navy in the Far East was authorization for the establishment of a strong naval base at Pearl Harbor.

Congress also continued to frustrate any moves directed at administrative reform within the Navy Department. Secretary Meyer took a big step toward breaking up the disorganized power of the bureaus, by transferring control to a group of supervisory line officers who would report to the Secretary and furnish him with impartial advice. He established this "aide system" on his own initiative and then went to Congress for approval; it was denied. The system remained in effect until the next Administration, but, lacking legislative sanction, it was not very effective.

As far as Congress was concerned, this had been just another attempt to take away some of its own more-or-less absolute power over the Navy; and Congress always resisted any efforts to organize a Navy general staff. There were several reasons for this attitude, some more valid than others. One of the least valid was that it would be hard for Congress to exploit a well-organized Navy and a well-informed Secretary; one of the most valid was the lingering distrust of all things military, and the attendant reluctance to concentrate too much power in the hands of a few men who might, after the fashion in other countries, try to control more than just their own department of the government. The General Board was in no way a general staff: it had no authority, controlled no forces or funds, and could make its recommendations only to the Secretary.

In 1914, under a new Administration, the Navy made another attempt to establish a workable staff, but this was frustrated not only by the Congress but also by the Secretary of the Navy, Josephus Daniels. He did not like the aide system (which had been established by a political rival) and took every public opportunity to denounce it as "cumbersome." He was against the idea of any type of general staff because it had too much the flavor of European militarism. (An entry in Admiral Fiske's diary of October 20, 1914 read: "Sec. gave out statement saying General Staff not consonant with principles of this Republic! Gosh!") Daniels, under pressure from some naval officers and some members of Congress, permitted the establishment of a Chief of Naval Operations; this officer was placed in theoretical control of all military functions of the Navy. But to satisfy Daniels and the rest of the Congress the position had to be defined in such a manner that the Chief of Naval Operations emerged as little more than a figurehead for the Navy and an errand boy for the Secretary.

President Taft's shipbuilding proposals had been frustrated, in part, because his party lacked the backing of a majority of Congress. When the Wilson Administration came to office in March 1913, it brought with it a partisan majority in both houses of Congress and also a platform plank calling for a strong Navy—two things which should have benefited the Navy. But it also brought confusion. The Democratic Party had always been the "small Navy" party, and the Republicans had traditionally favored a "big Navy." With the election of Wilson, the small-Navy party was committed—at least on the surface—to promoting a large fleet, and the Republican opposition had to choose between support of their own long-standing programs (passage of which would now stand to the credit of the Democrats) and political partisanship.

The confusion proved to be greatest for the Democrats. The party split into two factions, one led by Congressman Richmond P. Hobson, who called for a navy in the Atlantic equal to that of Germany and a navy in the Pacific equal to Japan's. The other faction was led by

Midwestern and Southern Democrats who wanted no more big-ship programs at all. This latter group maintained that the present naval force was sufficient to any need, as the United States was hardly in danger of attack from any quarter. The Hobson group called attention to the nation's extended overseas commitments in the Philippines, in China, and in the protection of other Western Hemisphere nations under the provisions of the Monroe Doctrine. They pointed out, not unreasonably, that the navies of any potential enemies were rapidly being expanded and that, even if the present U.S. Navy might be sufficient, it must soon fall so far behind as to become once again insignificant.

The final result, in the first two years of the Wilson Administration, was a battleship-building program slightly more ambitious than that of preceding years: a total of five big ships were authorized. But a battleship program does not make a navy; and, as before, it merely stood as the symbolic token of the government's concern for the national defense. The Administration quickly proved that it was not really interested in the Navy and not disposed to use its majorities in Congress for the passage of beneficial—and necessary—legislation. The personnel shortages, for example, had become acute, but Secretary Daniels refused to acknowledge the existence of any shortage even though the General Board had set the deficiency at almost 20,000 men. In his annual report for the year 1914, Daniels stated that "wise utilization of the present personnel" would obviate the need to increase personnel ceilings. What he was actually proposing was a further reduction in the already inadequate manning levels of ships in commission. In its own report for that year, the General Board had included a recommendation for the 20,000-man increase— and Secretary Daniels refused to print the report until all reference to this specific shortage had been deleted. His only concession to the personnel situation was to approve establishment of a Naval Reserve, to be made up of men who had once served in the Navy. This was the year that saw Europe go to war. The first World War was a war that no one seriously thought would last more than a few months; a war that was the unfortunate (but not unexpected) result of a series of binding alliances between various nations in Europe; a war that was the logical outcome of the Anglo-German arms race; and a war that was triggered by the nationalistic impulses of some peoples and the nationalistic pride of all peoples. The official attitude of the United States was one of neutrality, but official actions tended to favor the Allies over the Central Powers.

When the war did not end by winter, and as the blood of 1914 flowed over into 1915, it worried observers in the United States that the favored combatants were not winning the anticipated glorious victory. It also became a matter of concern that the United States had taken no measures to prepare itself for a war that might well spread to its own shores. As a result, a well-organized "preparedness movement" grew up. This was not a crackpot movement, but was supported by many leading business and political leaders; the methods employed in whipping up interest in preparedness might have bordered on the sensational, but the men behind the movement were sincere.

The Germans, the public was led to believe, were soon to overrun the British and French armies and break out across all of Europe. The mighty German fleet would crush the British navy, brush aside the feeble U.S. Navy, and shell American seacoast cities to rubble in preparation for the landing of millions of brutally savage German soldiers for what would be, it was graphically emphasized, the "Rape of America." Propaganda of this nature appeared everywhere—in newspapers, magazines, books, advertisements, and motion pictures —and the palpable improbability of such an operation did not offset the fear created. Naval and military experts—who might be expected to have a vested interest in promoting any increase in the military departments—testified before Congress that the situation was in no way as grim as it was pictured in the public press. They cited the obvious difficulties that an enemy fleet must encounter in extended operations away from its own bases, and the extreme difficulties that would be faced by an enemy ground force attempting to land on a hostile shore.

The preparedness movement did, however, produce some results. The United States was patently unprepared for any extended or extensive military operations of its own, and, in spite of a hard-core reluctance on the part of the Administration to undertake any actions that might in any way appear to be belligerent in nature, some improvements were made. The General Board prepared a five-year plan for the orderly development of the Navy, and called for a fleet "equal to the most powerful maintained by any other nation in the world." Secretary Daniels thought that the language of this request was perhaps too strong, and rephrased it as "a navy worthy of this country and able to cope with any probable enemy." President Wilson was even more cautious, and asked for a navy that would be "incomparably the most adequate navy in the world"—whatever that meant—which could offend no one. But the General Board's program was submitted to Congress and was passed after heated debate with little amendment except that the time element was compressed to three years. It was the first time in her history that the United States had an organized plan for naval construction to replace the annual tug-of-war between military and political considerations.

The act of August 29, 1916 authorized 157 ships, 66 of them to be started immediately. Its provisions formed practically a navy in itself—ten battleships, six battle cruisers, ten scout cruisers, fifty destroyers, sixty-eight submarines of various types, three fuel ships, two destroyer tenders, two gunboats, two ammunition ships, a repair ship, a transport, a hospital ship, and a submarine tender. It was an ambitious program and, for a change, a balanced one.

Unfortunately, however, it was a program that was in no way geared to the type of war that the United States would soon be fighting and was, in fact, to be virtually suspended seven months later when the United States entered the war. The keel of the first of the sixteen capital ships had then just been laid down, when the Navy Department realized that it was unlikely that any of the big ships could be completed in time to see service in the war, and that, considering the size of the combined British and American battle fleets and the general lack of escort and support ships, the money and effort could more profitably be put into other construction. Accordingly, work was halted and the emphasis belatedly shifted to the building of destroyers and submarine chasers.

Belatedly, because prior to the United States' entry, if there was any clear lesson that could have been drawn from the conduct of the war, it was that any major contribution which the U.S. Navy would be called upon to make would be in antisubmarine warfare. Throughout the war, the German battle fleet was effectively out of action, bottled up in the North Sea by the British navy. The Allies were maintaining a tight blockade of the Central Powers—a blockade that was to have a decisive part in ending the war, for it virtually destroyed the enemy's ability to support troops in the field and at the same time to feed, clothe, and house the people at home. One early German attempt to break this blockade resulted in the Battle of Jutland, a massive encounter between elements of the two opposing fleets which ended in a paper victory for the Germans—their losses were only about one-half those of the British. But the British won a strategic victory: the German objective had not been achieved and the blockade was unbroken. The enemy fleet returned to port—and stayed there for the rest of the war.

As the fighting ground on through years of bloody stalemate, as stores, matériel, and provisions steadily dwindled, only one option remained open to the Germans—one hope of victory. This was to reverse the *status quo* and set up a tight blockade around the British Isles. Britain was even more dependent than Germany upon outside sources of supply, and this had always been her strategic weakness; therefore, the British had always maintained the largest navy in the modern world. Previously Germany had tried to counter this force in the traditional fashion, and failed. The Germans now shifted their emphasis to a new weapon—the submarine.

The submarine had always been regarded as a dangerous toy, more dangerous to its own crew than to any enemy. Submarine operations in the early days of the war reflected this attitude, but the submarine soon proved itself to be a valuable weapon. After the three British cruisers had been sunk by one German submarine—because the commanding officers of cruisers numbers two and three had stopped their ships dead in the water to rescue the survivors from cruiser number one—both sides gained a healthy respect for the little boats.

Submarine operations went through several cycles before the time of the United States' entry into the war. In the early months of 1915, Germany was holding to the concept that any ship which entered a specified and well-publicized war zone was fair game. However, the sinking of the Cunard liner *Lusitania* on May 7, with a large loss of life among the civilian passengers, including many Americans, raised a storm of protest. Although the ship was carrying some ammunition (and was possibly even armed as an auxiliary cruiser), and although the German government had pointedly warned through newspaper advertisements that anyone who traveled on the *Lusitania* would do so at their own risk, Germany was forced to apologize for the sinking and revise her program of operations. The German government agreed to demands that submarines must hold to the accepted rules of war: that fair warning must be given to any ship about to be attacked unless it was a warship, and that adequate provisions must be made for the rescue and safe passage of all crew and passengers.

But the rules of "civilized" warfare quickly proved to be loaded against the submarine. When German commanders attempted to give warning to a merchant ship, they frequently discovered—too late—that it was not a merchant ship at all, but a heavily armed decoy. Additionally, even the most innocent of vessels came to be armed with a deck gun or two, and the thin skin and necessarily low reserve buoyancy of the submarine made it exceptionally vulnerable to shell fire. It became a matter of survival for the submarine to attack first and be "humane" second.

By April 1916 German submarines were once again attacking everything that came into sight. This included a few American ships carrying on a brisk trade with Britain, and President Wilson was again moved to demand that Germany cease this unrestricted submarine warfare. If it did not, "the United States can have no choice but to sever diplomatic relations with the German empire altogether." Germany was not, at this point, willing to risk United States intervention in the war, and again agreed to adhere to the recognized principles of international law pertaining to the visit, search, and destruction of merchant vessels.

This pledge was kept for almost a year; but by December, the effects of the Allied blockade had become so acute that the German High Command determined that the only recourse was to launch a vast, unrestricted submarine offensive in order to force Britain out of the war. The Admiralty staff estimated that, if the offensive started on February 1, 1917, England would be starved out of the picture by the beginning of July and complete surrender of the Allies should occur by August 1. The probable effect of the United States' entry into the war as a result of this offensive was studied, weighed and, because of the short time span, determined to be of minimal consequence.

In a secret memorandum dated December 22, 1916, the Admiralty specified that the announcement of this campaign and the actual beginning should "follow so quickly one upon the other that there is no time for negotiations, especially between England and the neutrals. The wholesome terror will exercise in this case upon enemy and neutral alike." The German ambassador at Washington presented the formal declaration of unrestricted submarine warfare late in the afternoon of January 31; the offensive started the next morning. On February 3, the steamer *Housatonic* became the first American casualty of this campaign and diplomatic relations with Germany were severed.

There was now no doubt that war would come. The Navy moved to arm all American merchant ships, and a bill to this effect was introduced into the Congress. The House passed it, but a filibuster was staged in the Senate which held the bill until that session of Congress ended on March 4. Guns were put on the ships despite this lack of congressional sanction, and the Secretary made arrangements to shift the battle fleet to a newly established base at Yorktown, Virginia. This was to be the headquarters of the fleet throughout the war—a deepwater bay, with an entrance sufficiently narrow to be closed against submarines and adequately large to anchor the whole Navy.

The Secretary of the Navy personally had been blocking all the Navy's attempts to ready itself for war, lest the Administration be accused of hypocrisy—the Democratic platform for the 1916 Presidential elections had rested solidly on the premise that Wilson was keeping the country out of war. The 1916 shipbuilding program had been publicly justified as "normal" expansion unconnected with events in Europe. But even he finally acknowledged that it was time to prepare for war.

FOURTEEN

World War I: Operations at Sea

*America has always boasted that she could
find men to do anything. She is the prize
amateur nation in the world. Germany is the
prize professional nation in the world. Now,
when it comes to doing new things and
doing them well, I will back the amateur
against the professional every time, because
the professional does it out of the book and
the amateur does it with his eyes open upon
a new world and with a new set of circumstances. He knows so little about it that he
is fool enough to try the right thing.*
—President Woodrow Wilson, in an informal
address to the men of the fleet, Yorktown,
August 11, 1917

THE OPERATIONS of the Navy in World War I were not very spectacular in the sense that the battles of the previous war had been
spectacular; but they were far from dull and proved to be of im-
measurable importance in the winning of the war. It did, however,
take the Navy a while to really get into the war. Since there had
been no preparations before war was declared, not even in such
basic things as topping off supply allowances on ships that would
be expected to go overseas, they had to be made after the declaration. And some of them took time. It may seem incredible, but on

[158]

April 6, the date the United States formally entered the war, exactly one-half of the Navy's forty-four relatively new oil-burning destroyers, and 67 per cent of all Navy ships were in need of repairs. Thus, instead of going into wartime service, they went into the shipyards for an average stay of fifty-six days.

William S. Sims—now a rear admiral—was sent to England as a one-man fact-finding and liaison mission to make preliminary arrangements for cooperation with the British and to report back to Washington on conditions in the war zone. Actually, Sims had not been Secretary Daniels' first choice for the assignment; Rear Admiral Henry B. Wilson had been favored, but it was decided that his duties in organizing a western Atlantic patrol force were too important to be entrusted to anyone else, so Sims, who was president of the Naval War College, was sent instead. Sims was already a popular man in England; in 1910, in a rousing speech before a London audience, he had asserted that in the event of war the English could always count on their "kindred across the sea." The speech won him many friends in England, but it did not sit too well with the scrupulously neutral government of President Taft. Secretary of the Navy Meyer had felt it necessary to publicly reprimand Sims for speaking out on matters that were not the proper concern of a naval officer.

War had not yet been declared as the admiral and his aide sailed from the United States and therefore, at the direction of Secretary Daniels, they traveled incognito in the guise of two civilian tourists. Sims was advised not to make any binding commitments with the British, just to investigate and report.

The United States entered the war while his ship was at sea, and so the necessity for secrecy was removed. Sims plunged into his mission and quickly determined that the submarine menace was going to be the biggest problem of the war. He advised that the United States should immediately send all available patrol and escort craft to England where a shortage of such ships was acute. German submarines were sinking merchant ships at the rate of fifty a week, which should have been evidence enough that the situation was critical.

But the admiral's reports, when received at the Navy Department, were not given much weight. Public revelation of the rate of sinkings had been suppressed by the British, and the true nature of the submarine as a naval weapon had not yet made a dent in strategic plans that centered on the battle fleet. Mahan had discounted the submarine in his investigations because he did not think commerce-raiding was important, and the submarine was essentially a commerce-raiding ship. The inclusion of escort ships in building programs had envisioned their use in protecting the battle fleet against torpedo boats and submarines, not in independent operations in conjunction with merchant ships. Accordingly, they were built only in numbers in proportion to the size of the battle fleet.

To have carried out Sims's suggestion that all available escort ships be sent overseas immediately would have left the American battle fleet relatively unprotected. This would not have been disastrous—the fleet was to see little battle service during the war, and could easily have been left in the well-protected waters of Chesapeake Bay. But this fact had not yet impressed itself upon the strategic planners at the Navy Department, who also expected at any moment to see a fleet of German submarines begin operations along the Atlantic coast—operations against which "all available" escort ships obviously would be needed. In this, they failed to consider that Germany had very few submarines that were capable of extended long-range operations, and they based their whole reasoning on the fact that two submarines had visited Atlantic coast cities in 1916, thereby proving that it was possible for submarines to cross the Atlantic. As it later turned out, a total of five enemy submarines conducted operations in American waters during one four-month period in 1918. They sank a few ships—mostly fishing craft and coastal cargo carriers that were not equipped with radios and could therefore neither be warned nor give warning of the submarine operations—and completely failed to accomplish their primary mission, which had been to block the movement of troops and supplies to Europe. (They did succeed, however, in causing the usual panic among the civilian population; the Navy Department received over five thousand telegrams, telephone calls, and letters in the twenty-four-hour period following the first reported attacks, all demanding that the Navy "do something.")

A few destroyers were sent to England as a token contribution to the war effort, but additional support was only cautiously added until, after months of desperate pleas from Sims and the corroborative reports of foreign delegations at Washington, a few other Navy leaders were prompted to make short tours of the war zone to investigate conditions for themselves. From that point forward, anti-submarine efforts were given the top priority. Work on the capital ships of the 1916 program was halted and the construction of hundreds of destroyers and submarine chasers was begun.

A bit of a controversy developed between Sims and the British over the question of convoys. To Admiral Sims, and to a number of other American naval officers, well-organized and well-protected convoys of merchant ships were a basic measure to be adopted against the submarine offensive. But the British were opposed to the use of convoys for merchant ships. They were not unaware of the value of the convoy system—all troopship movements were escorted —but they did not feel that merchant ships could successfully be operated in concert. This was an opinion also shared by the merchant captains, who did not feel that their ships or crews were suited to steaming in close formation with ships of dissimilar types, especially at night with all ships running darkened, and in fog or rain. Their apprehension was not unreasonable, but they never really gave the system a trial. The British relied upon wide dispersion of merchant ships traveling independently, with a heavy concentration of random warship patrols in the danger zone. (The danger zone could be calculated with a fair degree of accuracy, given the known capabilities of German submarines and the known areas where surface traffic would necessarily be heavy, as in the final approaches to a harbor.) This procedure, however, was obviously not preventing the Germans from sinking merchant ships at a rate far in excess of shipbuilding output.

Opinion in the United States was mixed, since some naval leaders favored the British system of patrols over a convoy system. But patrols resulted in grossly inefficient utilization of patrol ships, and since patrol ships were in short supply, the convoy was a logical step. Another possible approach—and this one was favored by President Wilson—was to attack the submarine bases and "shut up the hornets in their nests." But both the Americans and the British agreed that this would entail too much risk.

The first attempt at mercantile convoy was tried by the British, at the United States urging, in May of 1917; it proved successful, and the convoy was applied wherever possible to subsequent movements. Most convoys were accompanied by at least one cruiser or battleship as protection against surface raiders; due to the shortage of escort ships, the convoys were joined by destroyers only in the danger zones. The system proved highly valuable, and the rate of sinkings dropped off sharply.

In general, the entire American naval effort was directed toward the safe transportation of troops and supplies from the United States to various ports in Europe. It was an effort that was launched from a standing start with no advance preparation, few trained personnel, and few readily available ships; yet it was an effort that must, at the very least, be characterized as magnificent. And it was not seriously compromised by the initial errors in judgment made by the Navy Department.

The German High Command, in discounting the effect of the American entry into the war, had maintained that there were neither enough ships nor soldiers available to have any impact on the fighting in Europe before the submarine offensive would have succeeded in forcing Britain out of action. But if there is any one native American genius, it is in doing impossible things in an incredibly short time. Millions of tons of merchant ships were built, and over 800 small warships—destroyers, submarine chasers, submarines, minecraft—

were constructed and put into service. The shipbuilding industry finally recovered the sophistication it had lost in the doldrums following the Civil War and was able to achieve some minor miracles. For example, Mare Island Navy Yard launched a destroyer 17½ days after the keel had been laid and had it ready for commissioning in a total time of 70 days; an east coast civilian yard had a destroyer ready for trials in 45½ working days. The prewar norm for construction time had been over one year.

By the summer of 1917, all available shipbuilding facilities were saturated with orders, and the Navy wanted to build an additional 150 destroyers. The government offered to assist private shipbuilders by financing and/or constructing whatever additional facilities might be required; shipyards seemed to spring like mushrooms from every tidal mud flat, and within a few months the destroyers were sliding down the ways. The magnitude of the destroyer program was immense; by the end of it, the Navy had 267 new destroyers at an investment greater than the cost of all the ships available at the beginning of the war.

The success of the shipbuilding programs was in large part due to the work of the Naval Consulting Board, which had been established in 1915 with Thomas A. Edison as its head. Membership was drawn from twelve leading scientific societies, each of which nominated two representatives to serve. The early work of the board centered on a thorough survey of the war-production potential of United States industries, in which such things as machinery, availability of material resources, and the location of skilled and semiskilled labor pools were noted. When the time came for industry to go on wartime footing, the information compiled by the board proved invaluable. It also had a worthwhile side result: it was important that the immediate patriotic impulses of skilled workers to go off and join the Army or Navy be curbed lest the production effort be impaired by a lack of personnel. The Consulting Board survey helped to identify workers in the most critical skills, that they might be persuaded to stay on the job in industry.

Another source of ships turned out to be Germany herself. When the war in Europe had started in 1914, over one hundred German and Austrian ships had put into American ports to wait out the duration of the conflict. Here, they were safe from enemy action, and if the United States should someday enter the war, the crews had detailed instructions to disable the machinery so completely that the ships would be of no use to the Americans. Secret orders to carry out these instructions were issued by the German ambassador a few hours before the resumption of the unrestricted submarine warefare, and the crews immediately began smashing condensers; cracking cylinder walls; putting sand, ball bearings, and scrap into engines; running boilers without water, etc. To have rebuilt every broken engine and burned out boiler would have taken years, and the Germans knew it. But they had not counted on Yankee ingenuity; by using every short-cut and patchwork method conceivable—welding, bolting, and wiring the machinery together—Navy experts had many of the ships ready for service in a few months.

During the war fourteen of these ships were used as cargo carriers and twenty others were put into the business of transporting American troops—in point of fact, actually carrying over one-half of all troops sent on American ships. The biggest windfall to the program had been the liner *Vaterland,* the largest ship in the world. Renamed the *Leviathan,* this 58,000-ton monster was so large that the United States had no drydock big enough to accommodate her and the British had but one—and that could only be used when the tide was exceptionally high. There was some opposition in the United States to using such an obviously prime target as a troopship, and it was correctly surmised that the Germans would be especially eager to sink her. But *Leviathan's* capacity of almost 10,000 troops was the decisive factor, and she made her first crossing of the Atlantic under U.S. control in December 1917. It was only her fourth crossing since she had been built. In the next eleven months, the *Leviathan* was to carry over 96,000 troops to Europe and be attacked several times by submarines, but without receiving any damage.

[164]

It was not enough, of course, to build or acquire a large number of ships; it was also necessary to enlist, equip, and train the men to run them. Within a period of eighteen months the Navy absorbed twenty-two times as many men as had served in the Spanish-American War; four times as many as had been in the naval service during the entire Civil War. Most of the 500,000 men were enlisted as members of the Naval Reserve Force, which had numbered only a few hundred at the beginning of the war; 10,000 men came from the State Naval Militia, 4,000 from the Coast Guard, and some from the Lighthouse Service and the Coast and Geodetic Survey. For the first time in history, women were taken on active duty to do clerical and stenographic work as members of the Reserve Forces—they served as Yeoman (F) in the Navy and Marinettes in the Marine Corps. The Army, which only a few years before had practically foundered in an attempt to supply a force of 250,000 men, rose to a strength of 4,000,000.

Assuming control of so many men brought with it many responsibilities, and these included, to the Secretary of the Navy, moral guidance. But he was not satisfied to merely guide; he made morals a matter of legislation. As he so primly phrased it, "The Administration at Washington charged with the conduct of the war, early realized that health was the foundation of military efficiency, that health was dependent upon clean living, and that the protection of men in uniform from drink and disease was the prime duty owed to them, to their parents, and to the world, dependent, in the last analysis, upon their fitness to fight. Ignorance, intemperance, and indifference were the first foes to be faced in 1917." Whatever the merit of his argument, he made himself resoundingly unpopular by having it made illegal for anyone to serve an alcoholic drink to any Navy man—whether in a public tavern or a private home. It was a law, we may presume, more honored in the breech than in the keeping.

The naval war at sea was essentially amorphous. There were no battles with which to mark the progress in the pages of a history, just

[165]

hundreds of skirmishes with submarines encountered in hundreds of thousands of miles of patrolling while moving millions of men across the ocean. The movement of troops and supplies and the protection of the convoys was a massive coordinated effort which was so successful as to be almost dull, and is perhaps best examined by a brief survey of the component forces.

DESTROYERS. The first naval units sent into the war zone were six destroyers which sailed from the United States under sealed orders on April 24. When 50 miles out at sea, the orders were opened and were found to be quite simple: Proceed to the British naval base at Queenstown (now Cobh) and report for duty; cooperate with the British, or the French, as appropriate. Even though this was but a token force, it was enthusiastically received by the British. The squadron's chief, Commander Joseph K. Taussig, won the immediate admiration of the senior British naval officer at Queenstown. Vice Admiral Bayly asked, "When will you be ready to go to sea?" Commander Taussig replied, "We are ready now, sir, that is, as soon as we finish refueling." The ships were given a few days' rest, and were actually sent out on patrol within four days of their arrival.

Destroyers made over two hundred attacks on submarines, with possibly four to six sinkings credited and at least seventeen U-boats forced to return to port for repairs. There may have been others; positive evidence to credit sinking of a submarine was difficult to obtain. An oil slick on the surface, perhaps a few bits of cork, some bubbles breaking gently from below—these signs could either mark a grave or merely indicate that a shrewd commanding officer was trying to throw his pursuers off the track. Destroyers captured one U-boat, which had been damaged by a depth-charge attack and forced to the surface, but it was not long in the United States' possession as the crew had opened the sea valves and the boat sank while the destroyer *Fanning* was attempting to take her in tow.

American destroyers operated in the war zone for six months without receiving any damage from the enemy, but on October 15, the *Cassin* took a torpedo in the stern. The ship was able to return to port under tow, and suffered only one personnel casualty—Gunner's Mate Osmond K. Ingram who, when he spotted the torpedo heading for the ship, had attempted to jettison the depth charges on the stern. He was killed, but for his heroism he was posthumously awarded the Medal of Honor. He also became the first enlisted man in the history of the U.S. Navy to have a ship named in his honor, the destroyer USS *Osmond Ingram* (DD-255).

In all, only two American destroyers were lost during the war—and one of those after being accidentally rammed by a steamer. The destroyers easily earned their class sobriquet of "workhorses of the sea" with some ships steaming over 65,000 miles a year in combat operations.

ARMED MERCHANTMEN. Armed guards of from sixteen to thirty-two men, normally under the command of a chief petty officer, were furnished to 384 ships that were not otherwise manned by naval personnel. They successfully repulsed 193 submarine attacks, frequently engaging in running gun battles with the enemy. One of the longest of these attacks lasted four hours—the German submarine fired 225 rounds, the steamer *Luckenbach* returned 202, and the fight was only broken off by the appearance on the scene of a destroyer.

Submarine commanders would frequently elect to surface and try to sink a ship with gunfire, which was far less costly than using torpedoes but was of course more risky. But even if the U-boat chose to launch a torpedo attack, it would have to be at periscope depth and the armed guards were sometimes able to stall off the attack by preventing the boat from remaining at periscope depth long enough to get a solution to his firing problem until the intended victim had steamed out of range. The low submerged speed of the U-boat prevented a stern chase. Only 31 of the 384 armed ships were sunk by the enemy—29 by torpedo, 2 by gunfire.

CARGO SHIPS. The Navy operated 450 cargo ships and lost 18—8 to mines or torpedoes, 4 to collisions, and 6 to other accidents. Four of these losses occurred after the war had ended.

[167]

TRANSPORTS. Two million American servicemen were transported overseas, almost half of them being carried on American ships. The others traveled in British, French, and Italian ships with their passage paid for by the United States. The U.S. Navy handled 82.75 per cent of all troopship escort duties, and after the war could justifiably boast that not one soldier aboard a troop transport manned by the U.S. Navy lost his life through enemy action, and not one troopship under American escort was sunk on the way to Europe. Two British transports were sunk en route with American troops; and five transports—two British, two U.S. Navy, and one manned by the U.S. Army—were sunk while returning empty to the United States, with small loss of life.

BATTLESHIPS. Some American battleships were assigned to serve with the British Grand Fleet, but saw little action as the German surface fleet could not be tempted out of port. Various ruses were tried—sailing unprotected convoys, sending inferior forces out to sea—but without success. Operations, however, were not at all casual: steaming during the winter months in a latitude equal to that of Alaska, in heavy seas with visibility obscured by freezing rain and snow and darkness lasting up to eighteen hours a day was a challenge to both men and machines. Opportunities for recreation were few, and the maximum liberty granted when the ships were in port was for a period of four hours—daylight hours only.

American battleships were attacked by submarines on six occasions, and the only damage suffered was that apparently caused by a submarine which got fouled in the starboard propeller of the *New York*. Two blades were broken off, and the battleship had to be dry-docked for repairs. The fate of the U-boat was never determined. The only large United States warship lost during the war was the armored cruiser *San Diego*, which struck a submarine-planted mine off Fire Island, New York, in July 1918.

The other concentration of capital ships was at Yorktown, Virginia, where they constituted a reserve force in readiness and acted as a training fleet for some 45,000 officers and men, most of whom were subsequently assigned to ships operating in the war zone.

SUBMARINES. Allied submarines were perhaps the most effective antisubmarine weapon; about 100 boats were credited with sinking 20 enemy submarines (which may be compared with 34 U-boat victims of some 500 destroyers, mostly British). American submarines were definitely credited with only one U-boat, but very few United States submarines were deployed in the war zone.

SMALL SHIPS. A large number of miscellaneous types of small craft were put into service—yachts were converted for inshore patrol duties, fishing boats were used as minesweepers, and hundreds of submarine chasers and minecraft were built. There were some losses among these ships—to weather, mines, submarines, and accident—but they made a good showing, especially when it is considered that they were manned almost entirely by reserves. Less than 1 per cent of the officers were Naval Academy graduates; only 5 per cent of all men were experienced sailors.

The most useful of these smaller ships was the 110-foot submarine chaser, designed by Naval Constructor J. A. Furer. They were small, and undeniably undermanned and underequipped, and were considered by some experts to be incapable of crossing the stormy Atlantic. But they quickly proved their worth; 340 of them were built and manned by Americans, and others were built for the Allied navies. One Navy Department official had originally thought that these boats were too large; Assistant Secretary of the Navy Franklin D. Roosevelt proposed building a large fleet of 50-foot boats, and became involved in a rather heated discussion with Furer on the matter. The General Board was asked to mediate the dispute, and voted for the larger craft.

Another design, a 200-foot boat known as the *Eagle*-class craft, was put into construction by Henry Ford, but the war ended before very many had been built.

[169]

William S. Sims was promoted to full admiral and placed in charge of all U.S. naval forces in Europe, with headquarters in London. He was, in general, responsible for coordination and cooperation with the British, for operations in British waters, and for the overall supervision of the 370 ships, 80,000 officers and men, and 45 bases that the U.S. Navy was to have in Europe before the end of the war. But the center of naval activity was in France, where most of the escort ships were based and where port facilities were developed or enlarged to handle the incoming troops and the vast bulk of supplies needed to sustain them at the front. An efficient organization controlled convoy routing and arranged rendezvous with escort units—since there were never enough escorts available to accompany each convoy back and forth across the Atlantic, except troop movements, a detailed schedule had to be maintained. Convoys returning to the United States were escorted through the danger zone, then detached to proceed unescorted while the destroyers picked up an eastbound convoy. Any errors or unexpected delays could seriously compromise the safety of the ships, because the destroyers' limited fuel capacity would not permit them to make long transits from detachment point to rendezvous, nor wait at sea for a tardy group. The Navy in France also handled stevedoring and transshipment of matériel in cooperation with the U.S. Army, inshore patrols and minesweeping in French waters, and communications. The use of radio added a new dimension to wartime command and control: any unit at sea could be contacted at any time to be warned of submarine activity, notified of a change in scheduled rendezvous, or ordered to the scene of an attack.

American ships saw service in many areas of the world. Although the fighting in western Europe took most of the headlines, Allied forces were operating in southern France, Italy, North Africa, Egypt, Palestine, and Greece—and all needed to be supplied. One-fourth of all Allied shipping passed through the Straits of Gibraltar. Navy units were also employed in the Pacific, and in Arctic waters—and, as it happened, not all of the fighting was with the Central Powers.

Most notable was the involvement of the U.S. Navy in the Russian Revolution.

Russia had been fighting with the Allies, but as a result of the 1917 Revolution the Bolshevik government entered into a treaty with the Germans that ended Russian participation in the war. Fifty million dollars' worth of supplies which had been furnished to the Russians were piled up at the port of Arkhangelsk, and were in danger of falling into German hands. Accordingly, the cruiser *Olympia*—Dewey's old flagship—was sent into northern waters with a small detachment of British troops to mount guard over the matériel. The local Bolsheviks were not happy to see the *Olympia* and made some halfhearted attacks on the Allied contingent, but with little success.

At about this same time, a German submarine sank a ship which some Russian naval officers—who were not exactly reconciled to the new government—had been using to collect sealskin for their own profit, with the loss of the cargo and most of the crew. The officers were prevented from any active participation in the war by the treaty, but the desire for revenge burned so deep that they turned over their entire force of three destroyers to Allied control—one to the British, one to the French, and one to the Americans on the *Olympia*. Thus a warship with the improbable name of *Karitan Yurasovsky* served as a unit of the U.S. Navy, manned half by Russian and half by American sailors.

Other groups of American sailors had several skirmishes with the Bolsheviks at Murmansk, Arkhangelsk, and on Lake Onega, where two armed motorboats manned by U.S. Navy men were cautiously engaged by Russian gunboats on three occasions. On the Asian front, a joint British-Japanese-Chinese-Czechoslovakian-American patrol force kept order in Vladivostok. That important port city had been captured from the Bolsheviks by a large group of Czech soldiers who had been trapped in Russia by the revolution and had been forced to fight their way all across Russia to the east coast of Siberia that they might be able to find transportation back home.

American inventors were to provide the Allies with a number of new weapons—or improvements on old weapons—that were to play an important part in the war at sea. The Naval Consulting Board served as a clearing house for suggestions from unofficial sources, and during the war screened over 100,000 ideas. Secretary Daniels, in his instructions to the board, had said, "Let no idea, however simply or roughly presented, pass unnoticed; often from the most unexpected source the highest value may be obtained." It was like opening Pandora's box: suggestions were sometimes received at the rate of 3,000 per week, and many of them dealt with technical matters that required careful and detailed study.

And many of them, as might be expected, were obviously impractical. About 80 per cent of the ideas were in the field of anti-submarine warfare, and among the most popular subjects were devices to ward off torpedoes or designs for unsinkable ships. There were over 1,500 suggestions for torpedo shields for merchant ships—including fixed, towed, and self-propelled models and at least one proposal for a porcupine ship with a thousand 50-foot spikes extending from the hull to detonate torpedoes or mines before they were close enough to do any damage. There were a number of suggestions for magnetic torpedo-deflectors—and as an example of the lack of technical sophistication of the average submission, the calculations for the magnetic field proposed in one of these suggestions were checked by the Bureau of Standards and were found to be in error by a factor of 640,000,000. The designs for unsinkable ships were just as imaginative, and all worked out to about the same thing: a relatively unsinkable ship would be easy enough to build (for instance, take a wooden hull and fill it with lumber), but it would have no room for any cargo.

Yet out of the mass of letters, telegrams, pamphlets, and in-person presentations, came a few solid ideas that developed into highly valuable devices or helped in the improvement of a previously mediocre weapon. One of the most useful of these was an anti-submarine listening device, whereby a surface ship could detect the machinery and propeller noises of a submerged submarine at a respectable distance.

Attempts to perfect such a device had been made in the early 1890's, but with indifferent results—the noise of the ship using the contraption invariably blotted out any external noises. Adding a directional feature proved to make the difference between failure and success, and the accepted design was essentially a physician's stethoscope connected to a U-shaped tube mounted under the hull of the ship. By turning the tube—which lay parallel to the surface of the water—the sound of a submarine could be localized on a given line of bearing. Two or three patrol ships working in concert could thereby obtain a fairly accurate estimate of the submarine's position, and head in for a depth-charge attack. The device was quite sensitive. One American submarine chaser which had a U-boat disabled on the bottom could hear the repeated attempts of the crew to restart the engines. And could hear, after the boat had been down for a day and a night, what sounded like twenty-five successive pistol shots. And then silence.

Depth charges were another addition to the naval arsenal, invented by the British and improved by the Americans. They had come into being after one frustrated British skipper reported that he had located a submarine, but the enemy had submerged and taken up a position under his ship. "If we only had some sort of bomb that we could shoot down into the water," an officer at headquarters is reported to have said . . .

The depth charge was a simple weapon, a can of explosive with a pressure-actuated firing mechanism that could be set to go off at a desired depth of water. By dropping random patterns, with charges set for various depths, a large volume of ocean could be filled with potent shock waves highly destructive to the flimsy and delicately balanced submarine. One improvement was the Y-gun, which fired charges out from the sides of the patrol ship to complement those rolled off from the stern.

Perhaps the most effective invention of the war was the antenna mine. Mines of various types had been around for many years, but had never achieved much distinction. It took too many individual mines to adequately cover a large area for them to be employed in

[173]

other than shallow coastal waters or in the entrances to harbors and rivers where high concentration could reasonably be achieved. It had been suggested early in the war, for example, that the northern entrance to the North Sea should be closed off with a mine barrier, thus blocking the one route that most U-boats must take to reach the shipping lanes without running the gauntlet of the English Channel. But the North Sea was 250 miles wide and up to 600 feet deep across the northern entrance, and to have even sparsely covered this with mines would have required a quantity of explosives in the neighborhood of 400,000 units—well beyond the industrial capacity of the Allies. The British made a few attempts, but abandoned the effort after "bitter and expensive" experience.

Then the Americans entered the war and, bringing with them fresh technology and a great productive capacity, developed a mine that could cover the area with only 70,000 units. This was an anchored mine with a long copper wire antenna suspended above it from a small float, which could be exploded from the electrical reaction between the copper of the wire and the iron of the hull of any ship brushing against it. The ship would not have to actually contact the mine itself, as was the case with previous designs, and one mine could therefore provide coverage through a greater depth of water. The British were at first reluctant to reopen the North Sea project, but eventually agreed to cooperate in a joint effort using the new mines.

The minefield was more easily laid down than had been thought possible. The first day of the operation—June 8, 1918—3,400 mines were placed in a string 47 miles long; one of the minelayers dropped a mine every 11½ seconds for more than two hours, without a break. The Northern Mine Barrage was completed by October 26, a deadly belt over 230 miles long and from 15 to 35 miles wide. It was a smashing success; even though not begun until late in the war and not completed until the war was almost over, the Northern Mine Barrage was credited with the sinking of 17 of the 200 German submarines lost during the whole four years of the war. It also came to have a strong psychological effect upon the U-boat crews, who at times had to be forced to make the transit of the field at gunpoint. The barrage cost about 80 million dollars, a large sum, but when one considers that over an extended period the U-boats had been sinking 70 million dollars' worth of ships and supplies each month, the cost was cheap indeed.

With the end of the war, the job of the mine force was only half finished. They had to go back and sweep up all of the mines they had laid. Because of various factors, and primarily because of the weather, sweeping operations did not begin until April 1919. They continued to the end of September, and proved to be one of the most hazardous undertakings of the war: twenty-three minesweepers were damaged, and eleven men killed.

FIFTEEN

World War I: Operations Ashore

Retreat, hell. We just got here.
—Colonel Wendell C. Neville, USMC,
Belleau Wood, June 1918

THE MASSIVE ARMIES of Europe had gone forth to do battle full of confidence, courage, and ignorance. Years had gone by and they had clashed furiously against each other—and achieved nothing, except the decimation of a generation. The fighting was not confined to any one area of the world, but it was the activity on the western front that was most significant and which is best remembered today. It was here that the fighting was bloodiest, the casualties the highest; and it was here that the majority of American forces were committed to break the stalemate.

The trench warfare of World War I is dimly preserved in books and movies and in the memories of those men who lived through it; but it is hard today to realize the terrible psychological impact it had upon the combatants. The deadlock on the western front lasted through most of the war, with the opposing armies often separated by a no-man's land between trenches that was little wider than the average city street. A constant fire was maintained, big guns and small, and through this steady rain of instant death and lingering disfigurement, all organized (or otherwise) attempts to break the stalemate proved disastrous. The casualty rate was high; the average length of service in the trenches was about five months before a wound sent a man back to the rear or, in one out of four instances, killed him. More than half of the ground forces were eventual casualties. In the major European armies, at least one man in ten did not survive the war.

Those men not wounded or who returned to the trenches were subject to steady psychological deterioration brought on by the shelling; by the fear of gas; by the constant stench of rotting flesh out in no-man's land; by the fat and fearless rats that lived alongside in the trenches; by the rains that would not soak into the earth but remained in deep mud and deeper pools because the natural drainage systems were destroyed by the artillery fire; by the machine gun, against which the finest of traditional military training offered no solution. Men learned that a bayonet and a splendid uniform were not a shield against death; but the leaders never did learn the tactics required by the new weapons. The slaughter went on for years, and neither side was receptive to overtures for peace.

The arrival of fresh, eager American troops broke the stalemate and tipped the balance of victory to the Allied forces. Yet the war did not end in a day; the words "Lafayette, we are here" (first uttered by Pershing's deputy, Charles E. Stanton, during the wreath-laying ceremonies at Lafayette's tomb, July 4, 1917) made good newspaper copy but did not reflect a presence of any immediate practical value. The first American troops arrived in June: a contingent of naval aviators early in the month, then a headquarters unit for the Army, followed by the first ground forces near the end of the month—the Army and a battalion of Marines. (The Marines served as part of the Army, since the Navy envisioned few requirements for large Marine units in naval operations. Some high-ranking Army officers objected to absorbing the Marine Corps, for the time being, but the Secretary of War did not have such a parochial viewpoint and gladly accepted Marine participation.) But the forces had to be organized, equipped, and trained, and this was to take time. The first American shots were fired at the Germans on October 23; no United States troops were involved in a major action until the following May.

The American Expeditionary Force (AEF) was under the command of General John J. Pershing, a tough, experienced soldier who refused to allow his judgment to be swayed by political pressures from home or by international considerations closer to the front. One of the biggest continuing problems with which he had to deal was a series of attempts by the French and the British to have American troops integrated into their units; scattered, that is, all along the front like so much cannon fodder. Pershing's goal was an American army, even if occasionally under the command of a foreign general, fighting as a unit in itself. And, where possible, fighting according to Pershing's assessment of the situation, not under the stultifying and obviously unsuccessful "rules" of trench warfare. (When the French heard that Pershing was training his troops in the art of riflemanship, and actually conducting target practice, they politely but forcefully suggested that the Americans should confine their training to the needs of trench warfare: the bayonet, the grenade, the mortar, the machine gun—and the shovel. Pershing ignored the suggestion.)

As American divisions were trained, they were moved into defensive sectors in the trenches. Training then continued under the tutelage of the enemy, who made a point of concentrating their efforts against the green troops. By the end of May, after several months of minor skirmishing, the French, who commanded in the area where the American troops were employed, conceded that some American troops were sufficiently trained to launch an assault against a German-held village. The assault was successful; the Americans withstood three German counterattacks and held the ground they had taken. This won for them the grudging admiration of the French, but apparently did not immediately impress the enemy. In assessing the operation, German headquarters attributed their failure to recapture the village to a lack of timing and organization, rather than to any particular tenacity or skill on the part of the Americans.

But German attention was being directed toward a major planned assault of their own, and they were little concerned with an isolated action in an unimportant village. This assault was to be directed against Paris—not for the capture of that city, but as a ruse intended to force a relocation of Allied forces all along the front so that a strong German force could drive through a weakened point and push on to the Channel.

The attack was well planned and the preparations were conducted in complete secrecy (although an American intelligence officer had made a few educated guesses and tried, without success, to convince the French that a German attack would be made in this particular sector). The enemy also used seasoned, well-trained soldiers instead of the collection of old men and young boys who had been holding the trenches. It began on the morning of May 27—300,000 Germans swarmed over the French lines and easily reached a position that was only an hour away from Paris. As a feint the operation was a failure, for the Supreme Allied Commander Marshal Ferdinand Foch recognized it for what it was and did not shift his reserves to cover the movement. However, the intended feint suddenly blossomed into an overwhelming victory, and the Germans pushed forward. The only available reserve forces were the not-quite-trained Americans, but there was no time for quibbling.

The American Second Division, composed of twin brigades of Regular Army and Marines, was moved to the front in French busses at the town of Château-Thierry. The United States government paid the fare; one French transportation officer delayed the movement of some Marine units because he insisted on obtaining an accurate head count of all passengers.

The French were in command of this operation, and it would be safe to say that a serious communications problem developed. The French commanders changed the orders to the American units so frequently that no one really knew where they were going, or even where they had been. Another difficulty—one that was to occur on several occasions during the war—was that the French sometimes placed American units in between French units, without benefit of interpreter or liaison. A frequent result was that the French would withdraw (or fail to advance in accordance with plan) while the

Americans fought on, only to find themselves unexpectedly surrounded by the enemy.

As the Second Division moved toward the ill-defined front lines a few miles from Paris, they passed retreating Frenchmen who were engaged in wholesale looting of the French villages through which they moved. The Americans were startled; but the French were philosophic—if they did not loot, the Germans would.

It was the French plan to fall back, drawing the enemy after them, and then launch a counterattack. Actually, the French troops were in a rout and the enemy was pushing them back. It was an American suggestion to set a line of defense and hold it; and this they did. The first four hours of actual fighting were the most critical: the German advance was stopped, Paris was saved (and if Paris had fallen, the Allied cause might well have gone with it), and then the Germans were forced back. The names of Château-Thierry and Belleau Wood were emblazoned forever in the record of the Marine Corps to mark the action, which lasted for some three weeks but, after the first few hours, was of questionable tactical value.

Still, there was no doubt as to the bravery or skill of the Marines. In spite of French blunders (such as ordering units which were not supplied with either grenades or mortars to make an attack against a network of well-placed machine guns, and then leaving the units—without relief—in contact with the enemy for two weeks), the objectives were taken; and there were some side benefits from the action. The war-weary French, who had been at this business for some four years, were given fresh inspiration. The Marines were the heroes of the hour. They were not the only American troops engaged in the fighting at Belleau Wood, but thanks to a slip on the part of a censor, they were the only American forces identified in the press and subsequently in the imaginations of the people back home. This one-sided publicity was noticed by General Pershing but allowed to continue for a week before censorship was once again imposed. This served a purpose—it whipped the Army units into a positive fury to get at the enemy and prove that they were as good as the Marines.

The 8,500 Marines of the Second Division saw other fighting during the war—most notably at Soissons, St.-Mihiel, Mont Blanc, and in the Meuse-Argonne Valley—but the tone for all was set during those first three weeks in June. The American approach to battle—a free-swinging use of initiative on the part of the individual soldier rather than a slavish adherence to a precisely timed and organized plan, which had been the basic tactics during most of the war, and the American reluctance to give up any ground had a deleterious effect upon the morale of the enemy. To the Germans, the Americans had been an unknown quantity in the equation of war, one that had to be identified before the final solution. The Americans identified themselves, and it was not long before the tales of their prowess were circulating behind the German lines.

There were not many Medals of Honor passed out during the war; five were given to Marines for ground action in France. Men like Gunnery Sergeant Ernest A. Janson, who rushed an enemy force of twelve men that was about to set up five light machine guns, bayoneted the two leaders of the group, and forced the others to flee, abandoning their guns. Or men like Sergeants Louis Kukela and Matej Kocak, Corporal John H. Pruitt, and Private John Joseph Kelley, each of whom single-handedly attacked and destroyed machine-gun emplacements. The Germans never did quite understand how men with such obviously European names could be so wholeheartedly American.

There were also other heroes with the ground forces. Navy medical personnel assigned to the Marine Brigade did not spend all of their time at dressing stations and hospitals far behind the lines. There is proof enough of this in that six doctors, dentists, and corpsmen were awarded the Medal of Honor for their efforts in taking out or caring for wounded men while under heavy fire.

Perhaps, however, the nomination for the most persevering hero of the war in Europe must go to Navy Lieutenant Edouard V. M. Izac. His is a story that merits telling in some detail.

At 9:00 A.M., May 31, 1918, the transport *President Lincoln*, returning empty to the United States in an unescorted convoy, was

[181]

torpedoed by the German submarine *U-90*. The submarine had first sighted the group of ships about 1:00 A.M., and had used the cover of darkness to plot the base course of the zigzagging convoy, and then moved around the ships to take up a position to intercept. The *President Lincoln* was hit by three torpedoes and settled rapidly. The signal to abandon ship was given within twelve minutes. The crew took to rafts and lifeboats; and the *U-90* surfaced in their midst. The commanding officer of the submarine was under orders to take as prisoner the senior naval officer of any ship that he sunk and now, under gunpoint, picked up the first officer he sighted. Thus began the series of almost legendary exploits that was to bring Lieutenant Izac the Medal of Honor.

Izac was to be taken to Germany for interrogation, and while en route on board the submarine he learned many interesting details of U-boat operations; so interesting, in fact, that he determined to escape as soon as possible in order to pass the information along to Allied headquarters. This information could prove invaluable— comprising such items as the routes taken by the submarines when proceeding to and from patrols, points of rendezvous, some methods of resupply, and some of the tactics of evasion from surface attack. Izac made his first attempt to escape while the *U-90* was cruising on the surface in the narrow waters between Sweden and Denmark, but just as he was about to slip over the side and into the water the commanding officer of the boat grabbed him.

Lieutenant Izac was transferred to a repair ship, and then to a prison ashore, all the while picking up more bits of information. He was interviewed by several German officers, and relations were cordial. Again he was transferred, and at this next prison was treated to a rudimentary but sometimes effective method of psychological interrogation: an officer would be placed in solitary confinement for one day, then moved into a cell with another prisoner who spoke the same language. Under the assumption that the normal human impulse would be to talk, the room was well equipped with hidden microphones so that the Germans might be able to sit in on the con-

[182]

versation, thereby hoping to pick up something of military value. However, most of the prisoners—including Izac—were alert to this practice.

Izac planned several escape attempts during the three weeks he was at this intermediate prison, but none of them worked out. He was transferred to the next prison camp by railroad—and it was on this journey that he made his second actual attempt. While the train was moving at about 40 miles per hour, and when the two guards who were assigned to watch over him had slightly relaxed their vigilance, Izac dove through a small window and out on to the tracks.

It took the guards a few seconds to react and pull the emergency cord, and it took the train about 300 yards to come screeching to a halt. Izac landed badly, hitting his head and his knees on the rails and crossties; he was momentarily stunned. The guards jumped from the train and ran toward him, shooting as they came. Izac could not get away; in fact, he could barely walk, and was recaptured. The guards gave him a spirited beating and then forced him to run—or at least, to move as quickly as his injured knees would allow—for about five miles along the tracks to the prison camp that was the scheduled destination.

Here Izac was placed in the prison hospital, where his injuries were treated; later, he was given a court-martial (the proceedings, conducted entirely in German, were unintelligible to him) which sentenced him to two weeks in solitary confinement as punishment for the attempt. He came out of the cell thirty pounds lighter but even more determined to escape.

Three succeeding plans to escape were likewise thwarted, probably because word of them was passed to the Germans by the inevitable prison spies. The next plan was to prove successful, since it was not announced to any of the other potential escapees until the afternoon of the attempt. For this, Izac had long been collecting bits of material that might prove useful: screws removed from door hinges all over the camp; chains woven from wire taken from the fences surrounding the tennis court; tools, both stolen and manufactured. He found two long wooden planks that were used as markers at the tennis court and, with his screws and pieces of wood taken from the Red Cross food parcel boxes, he constructed an 18-foot-long bridge that could be laid from the window of his barracks, over the top of two parallel fences that surrounded the camp. Shoe polish was rubbed into the wood so that it would not show up in the darkness. Soon after taps on the night of the escape the prison electrical system was short-circuited with a length of the wire chain, and the bridge was moved into place. Lieutenant Izac and two other prisoners crawled across it and dropped to the ground outside the perimeter fence. They were noticed immediately by the guards, who realized that an escape was in progress when the lights went off; but it was a black and starless night, and the three men were able to run for cover.

Several other groups of men were involved in the escape, each group using a different method to get past the fences while Izac's group drew the fire of the guards. One group was to cut the fence with wire cutters, another to build a ladder to climb over the fences, and a third to rush through the main gate in company with the guards who would be expected to go forth in pursuit of the escapees (hopefully, this third group would not be noticed in the darkness and confusion). It is not known precisely how many of the other men were successful, but at least one man made it out through the gate and was able to join up with Izac about two miles from the camp.

These two men then began a walking tour of wartime Germany, headed for the Swiss border. For the most part, they subsisted on raw vegetables picked from the fields, and on the seventh night—having covered about 120 miles—they reached the Rhine River. The last leg of the journey was a midnight swim across the swift moving icy current, under the noses of German sentries. But the far bank was Switzerland; and they made it.

Izac was taken to London for an immediate debriefing by both the Americans and the British. He then was returned to the United States, arriving in Washington on the same day the war ended. The fact that his information was received too late to have any real effect upon the war—for the war had already been won—does not lessen the merit of his achievement. He was retired from the Navy in 1921 because of the injuries he had received while a prisoner, with the rank of lieutenant commander. Later, he became a member of Congress, where he served for ten years.

World War I also saw the emergence of a new breed of man— young, exuberant men, racing daily toward blazing glory or flaming death, and all of them were heroes. These were the birdmen; and prominent among them were the naval birdmen. The first of the American armed forces to land in France were naval aviators; and the first enemy plane shot down by an American aviator, March 19, 1918, went to the credit of the Navy.

Naval aviation entered the war with 48 officers and 55 aircraft (few of which were of any use). Congress—in a gesture of magnaminity that did not at all make up for the general lack of interest in aviation that had characterized previous appropriations—gave almost 800 million dollars to the Army and Navy for the purchase of airplanes. Unfortunately, there were no production facilities in the country capable of turning out airplanes on a scale sufficient to use up the money, nor were there any manufacturers really capable of turning out many good airplanes at all. Where the European nations had been vying with each other for years in the development of useful military airplanes, and as a result had produced an aggregate of some 150,000 of them, American manufacturers, lacking official encouragement, had lagged far behind.

Still, even though there were few planes, and even though many of those had to come from the Allied factories in England and France, American naval aviators succeeded in compiling an impressive record. Their primary mission was patrol, and 791,398 miles were flown on such duty—5,691 flights. Forty-three submarines were attacked, and at least two—and possibly four—of them were sunk. Another 18,000 flights were recorded in training, as the organization expanded to 2,000 pilots and over 2,000 planes, balloons, and dirigibles, with 38,000 additional officers and men assigned in support.

Aviators also flew a number of offensive missions, dropping bombs, strafing, cutting down observation balloons, and attacking enemy aircraft. The first U.S. naval ace was Lieutenant David S. Ingalls who, typical of the breed, flew three or four missions a day, on one occasion single-handedly attacking a flight of six enemy planes, shooting down one and driving the others away. (He was later to be appointed Assistant Secretary of the Navy for Air by President Hoover. Another world war naval aviator to achieve high appointive office was Navy Cross holder Robert S. Lovett, Secretary of Defense under President Truman.)

A representative mission was the one undertaken on August 21, 1918, by five seaplanes—a bomber and four escorts—based in Italy. Their objective was simple enough: to drop propaganda leaflets over Pola, an Austrian naval base. The Austrians, unmoved by the non-aggressive nature of the operation, sent up a barrage of antiaircraft fire and launched seven fighters to give battle. In the ensuing action, one of the American planes was severely damaged, and hot oil spraying from the punctured crankcase burst into flame. The pilot put his plane into a spin and the slipstream blew out the fire, but when he leveled off at about 1,500 feet he was attacked by one of the enemy and had to go into another spin to escape. He pulled out just above the water; his engine now finished off by the last attack, he was forced to land. He was three miles from the enemy base.

Three Austrian destroyers got underway and headed toward his plane and, just to keep things interesting, a fresh squadron of planes took to the air. Ensign George H. Ludlow took a moment to finger two bullet holes in his leather flying helmet (his scalp was grazed), and then opened the photographic port in the hull of his plane and began kicking holes in the wings, trying to sink the plane before the Austrians could salvage it.

In the meantime, back in the sky, his partners had managed to drive off the first enemy attackers, and two of the fighters and the bomber headed for home. The other fighter came down and landed

[186]

alongside Ludlow, who gratefully climbed aboard. Since the fighter was a single-place plane, Ensign Ludlow had to sit under the engine, hanging on to the struts for support; the pilot, Ensign Charles H. Hammann, somehow managed to get the overloaded plane airborne just before the destroyers arrived on the scene. He made a quick pass over Ludlow's plane, gave it the *coup de grâce* with a burst from his own guns, and then headed for home just far enough ahead of the fresh group of enemy planes to make good the escape.

The 60-mile flight to home base was uneventful, but the trip ended in a spectacular splash as the plane turned turtle on landing. Neither of the officers was seriously injured; and, for his efforts, Ensign Hammann became one of the two naval aviators awarded the Medal of Honor for combat operations in the war.

The other aviator was a Marine, Second Lieutenant Ralph Talbot. He won his medal in a fight against 6 to 1 odds on October 8, 1918, when his plane shot down two of the enemy and he managed to escape from the rest by flying across the German trenches at an altitude of 50 feet. His observer, Gunnery Sergeant Robert G. Robinson, was credited with one of the kills and also received the Medal of Honor for sticking with the fight even though he had been severely wounded.

Another branch of naval activity that acquired some degree of professional standing during the war was Naval Intelligence. Founded in 1882, this branch had gotten off to a slow start, largely because of public and military antagonism to such unsportsmanlike work as "spying." It had concentrated most of its prewar effort on the compilation of technical and statistical information about foreign navies. But the activities of Naval Intelligence from the time the war started in Europe were of a more covert nature, and the results often proved quite valuable. For example, the crews of the German ships interned in the United States did not really remain neutral during their stay; they engaged in such pastimes as manufacturing bombs—to be hidden on Europe-bound ships—with fuses set to explode when the ships were far out at sea. This plot was uncovered before any damage was done. One of the interned ships was also found to be serving as a clearing house and temporary hotel for persons who wanted to be smuggled into Germany from the United States.

After the United States had entered the war, agents worked closely with French authorities in organizing a network of fisherman-observers, who regularly reported on coastal U-boat activities in Europe. In the United States, German sympathizers and potential saboteurs were identified and prohibited from entering defense plants, dockside areas, and shipyards. Overseas cargoes consigned to neutral ports in Europe were checked for contraband—radio equipment, lubricating oil, machinery parts—which seemed to have a way of ending up in Germany. Counterespionage work also foiled the efforts of the military attaché to the German Embassy directed at persuading Mexico to enter into an alliance with Germany and make war plans against the United States; and the efforts of the naval attaché to supply German raiders with various supplies.

The Navy participated in a number of miscellaneous undertakings —such as the building of a 36-mile pipeline across Scotland so that ships of the Grand Fleet, on the east coast, could be supplied with fuel oil from tankers in much safer waters of the west coast. But the most unusual naval undertaking of the war was the operation of naval guns mounted on railway cars in France.

The reason behind this project was that German long-range guns had been reaching well into Allied territory and were virtually unassailable. Allied military planners wanted to obtain some artillery with a similar range (roughly 24 miles). This undertaking was, however, more for purposes of morale than for any specific tactical use, and in the summer of 1917, the U.S. Navy worked out a plan to mount some naval guns for use ashore.

While novel, the idea itself was actually not new. Guns taken from ships had been used in China, Mexico, and Africa in recent years, and both the Germans and Italians had used them in the current war. But most of these had been relatively light guns, pressed into service

[188]

under the exigencies of a given tactical situation. The new proposal envisioned using the largest guns available. (The standard 14-inch gun was selected as the largest practicable, even though some 16-inch guns had been manufactured, because barrels were in stock as ordnance spares for many battleships and this size ammunition was a regular item of supply.)

Work was begun in November. Special railway cars were designed for the guns themselves, and five of these were constructed. Support units, consisting of ammunition, machine shop, barracks, head-quarters, and communications cars were built, using standard rolling stock wherever possible. The units were all designed to be compatible with French roadbeds and equipment; the fittings and equipment (bunks, cook stoves, etc.) were taken from standard Navy stock. A total of eighty cars went to make up the five batteries and head-quarters unit; and a crew of thirty officers and five hundred men were selected to man them.

The completed batteries were too big to be sent overseas in assembled units, so they were broken down, to be reassembled at dockside in France. There were a few problems: the ships were loaded "upside down" with the carriage and the framework at the bottom and the accessories on top, so that all of the material had to be unloaded before the reassembly could begin. The blueprints had somehow become lost in transit so that the units had to be put to-gether from memory. Fortunately, members of the battery crews had been assigned to assist naval inspectors at the contractor's shops, and the work went smoothly enough. The first gun was assembled, tested, and moved into position for use against the enemy.

The batteries were designed to be fired from either an unprepared site, on a regular section of track, at angles of elevation up to 15 degrees; or from a prepared position over a reinforced pit that was needed to accommodate the recoil of the gun at angles of elevation from 15 to 43 degrees. For unprepared firing, recoil was absorbed by the backward movement of the railway car itself against the friction of the brakes. When over a pit, the car was set on jacks and made

[189]

rigid. It took slightly less than two days to prepare a site for firing.

The first combat use of the battery came on September 6, 1918, about a year after the idea was conceived. It marked the first firing of an American shell, from an American gun, manned by American gunners, in action on the western front. (The majority of guns used by the AEF during the war were of French design and manufacture —.75 mm. and .155 mm., primarily—because these guns were available and had a ready supply of ammunition at all points in Europe.)

The first shot was fired at a small town held by the Germans. It was the only shot fired that day, because the target was captured by the French immediately after the shell had landed. There was no direct connection, however—the town's capture had already been assured and was merely delayed a few minutes to allow the gun crew to make their initial contribution to the war effort.

The remaining four batteries were quickly assembled in turn and brought into action, and during the period from September 6 to November 11, a total of 782 rounds were fired by the guns. Accuracy of the flat-trajectory barrels was exceptional—evaluation of one target showed that 24 shells had landed within an area 302 yards by 102 yards. And this, at a range of 35,800 yards and after the barrel had already fired 150 times.

The railway batteries were considered to be a success. From an operational standpoint, they were quite effective. One well placed shell could take out three sets of railway track and roadbed for about 100 feet; one poorly placed shell is known to have uprooted ten acres of turnips, which gives a fair indication of the magnitude of the explosion. One shell landed in a movie house during a show, killing 40 German soldiers and wounding 60 more; another shell, which landed in a staff headquarters, possibly killed 70 soldiers.

But the greatest asset of the guns, which was definitely enhanced by their mobility, was the morale factor. This was negative when applied to the Germans—the thought of one of those big shells coming from out of nowhere, 15 or 20 miles behind the front lines, was absolutely demoralizing. The factor was positive when applied to the Allied troops and especially to the French peasantry, who had spent so many years under the shadow of death. The sight of the massive gun and its impressive train of support cars moving through the countryside was a definite boost, and the sight of American sailors so far inland was an interesting novelty. Moreover, since the guns moved around with relative ease, it always seemed to friends and enemies alike that there were more than five batteries.

Under ideal conditions, airplanes were used to spot the fall of shot. But because of the extreme ranges involved, the spotting plane would have to fly at an altitude of about 15,000 feet where the freezing air drastically cut into the pilot's efficiency, and where haze or mist—so light as to be imperceptible on the ground—could effectively block both the target and the gun from view. The planes were equipped with radio transmitters, but not receivers, and therefore had to be in a position to see both the target and visual signals from the battery. Large pieces of white cloth were laid out on the ground in various patterns to transmit data to the planes.

The usual method of firing these huge railway guns was through mathematical aim. The exact geographical position of the gun was determined by standard surveying techniques, which the Navy men easily picked up because of the similarity to celestial navigation and piloting. The relative position of the target would be determined using maps and, after applying corrections for direction and velocity of the wind, barometer reading, drift, velocity loss from erosion of the barrel and temperature of the powder, an appropriate direction and angle of fire were obtained. There were no sights on the guns (targets were never in sight from the guns anyway) but surveying instruments, used in conjunction with any fixed object, such as a church steeple, served to line up the battery.

The last shot from any of the guns was fired at 10:59 A.M., November 11, 1918. One minute later, the war was over.

SIXTEEN

The Naval Lessons of the
Great War

*The U.S. Navy is organized for defeat in the
Atlantic and would not have a chance
against any Asiatic power in any way, shape,
or form.*
—Brigadier General William L. Mitchell,
New York *Times*, February 14, 1922

ANOTHER WAR had ended; but not the work of the Navy. There was a
network of bases to be disestablished and some 400,000 men to be
demobilized. There were postwar disputes to be mediated and American property, as always, to be protected in Italy, Turkey, Greece,
and Yugoslavia. In addition, there were 2,000,000 soldiers who had
been carried to France and were now eager to return home. Every
available ship was pressed into this service: cargo ships were converted to troop carriers, captured German ships were put to immediate use; and even homeward-bound battleships and cruisers were
crowded with Army personnel who gladly accepted the discomforts
of traveling in a cramped warship to get home. A total of 142 ships
were eventually employed in this operation; even so, it took over ten
months to carry most of the troops back to the United States.

There were also awards to be presented to deserving officers and
men—medals for heroism, medals for outstanding performance, medals for helping to win the war. Commanders in the field submitted

[192]

their recommendations to the Navy Department, and an awards board consolidated the lists and made modifications where justified. The Secretary of the Navy made some recommendations and amendments of his own, sometimes without apparent justification, and thereby provoked a completely unexpected public controversy.

Admiral Sims was to have been awarded the Distinguished Service Medal (DSM), the highest award that could be given for administrative achievement. In his own recommendations, Sims had asked the DSM for a number of officers who had served on his staff in London. When the awards board and/or the Secretary downgraded thirteen of these recommendations to Navy Crosses, Sims was so outraged that he refused to accept his own DSM and publicly denounced the whole awards system. He chided Secretary Daniels for giving high awards to commanding officers of ships that had been sunk and not giving equally high awards to men who had "obviously" played a more important role in the war. Daniels responded by criticizing Sims for not having recommended any enlisted men for awards, and justified the awards to the torpedoed skippers on the reasonable ground that by their individual coolness in the face of disaster they had prevented additional loss of life.

The attendant publicity prompted the Senate to launch an inquiry into the whole matter. While no substantive changes were made in the awards as a result of the hearings, they did amount to something of a psychological victory for Admiral Sims. Secretary Daniels' method—or more properly, lack of method—in allocating awards, and his sometimes arbitrary revision of awards, stood clearly revealed. But the investigation was to lead directly into a more serious and potentially explosive inquiry—the role of the Navy Department in the conduct of the war itself.

Admiral Sims had been in the process of writing a scathing condemnation of the Navy's lack of preparation and lack of direction in the early months of the war, which was to be submitted as an official communication to the Secretary of the Navy. This letter just "happened" to come to the attention of one of the senators on the awards investigation committee, and a full-scale hearing was shortly convened on this matter.

The arguments contained in the letter "Certain Naval Lessons of the Great War," dated January 7, 1920, can generally be summed up as follows:

1. The Navy was not prepared for a war that was patently inevitable. There was a drastic shortage of personnel, the material condition of the fleet had suffered greatly as a result, and no effort had been made to improve conditions. The fleet was unbalanced, comprising too many battleships and not enough ships of other types without the support of which the battleships would be virtually useless.

2. The Navy had made no plans for mobilization, and had no plans that centered on antisubmarine and transport operations, even though it had been clearly demonstrated that these operations would be of prime importance should the United States enter the war.

3. There were excessive delays in executing what few plans that did exist. Valuable time was lost in formulating new plans. There was too much vacillation in the first six months of the war.

On these points, the evidence brought out in the hearings was in substantial agreement. Secretary Daniels himself was on record in many places as being opposed to any increase in personnel; he had not permitted any overt moves that would increase the readiness of the fleet until after war had been declared; he had not even made reasonable efforts to keep the fleet in a "normal" state of readiness. (For example, no gunnery trophy was awarded to destroyers in 1916 "because"—in the official explanation—"of the small number of vessels completing the year's work, and because the scores obtained by these vessels do not warrant the award of the trophy." No apparent attempts had been made to enforce gunnery training requirements.)

Sims's purpose had not been, however, to vilify the Secretary of the Navy in the person of Josephus Daniels, but was another effort to prompt a reorganization of the Navy, this time by winning public sentiment to the cause of reform by demonstrating that the present organization had not been adequate to keep the Navy in a state of readiness. But public sentiment was content to leave the war in the past—a war, after all, that had been won, a war in which the Navy had played an important role. Public sentiment, if any, turned the investigation into a duel between Sims and the Secretary, and the hearings became a dual personality contest and political football. A Presidential election was less than a year away, and the Republican majority on the committee was more than happy to uncover any evidence that might discredit the Democratic Administration. It was reasonably demonstrated during the hearings that the organization of the Navy was so constituted as to be potentially disastrous; that even the theoretical head of the Navy, the Chief of Naval Operations, had no power to ensure that the fleet was in a state of readiness or that it might be properly deployed in time of war. However, no change in Navy administration was to come about as a result of the hearings, which—as was the case in most such inquiries—ended with the issuance of a partisan and inconclusive report.

If, however, the Navy was not to be reorganized as a result of the "Lessons of the Great War," it at least had found in the war a new weapon which was to prove of great importance in future operations—the airplane. Aircraft had demonstrated their usefulness, especially in reconnaissance and patrol work, and the Navy proceeded to conscientiously develop the infant science of flying. One important advance to come directly from the war was a design for a long-range flying boat. It had been conceived in an attempt to create an airplane that would be capable of flying across the Atlantic (something that had not yet been done), thereby relieving overcrowded surface transportation of the burden of some high-priority cargoes. The first plane of this type, the *NC-1*, was completed in October 1918, and several sister ships followed soon after. The war ended before any saw active service, but six months later one of them—the famous *NC-4*—successfully spanned the Atlantic on a hopscotch route from Long Island to Nova Scotia to the Azores, to Portugal, and from there to Plymouth, England.

Another step forward came with the postwar decision to experiment with a ship for use as an aircraft carrier. The U.S. Navy had been the first to operate an airplane from a ship, but this had only been by way of demonstration. The British were the first to effectively combine the airplane and a ship into a combatant team, and other nations (most notably Japan) were known to be working in this area. In 1919, the General Board recommended that at least one ship should be adapted to aircraft operations in order to fully test out this concept, and Congress was in agreement. The collier *Jupiter* was selected for the conversion; a collier was preferred over other types of ship for several reasons. It was available, due to the fact the Navy's coal-carrying business was rapidly dropping off as more and more of the fleet became oil-burning. And colliers had large holds, high decks, large hatches—all of which would permit easy handling of aircraft—and required a smaller crew to operate than combatant-type ships. The conversion was completed in 1922, and the *Jupiter*—re-named the *Langley* in honor of the aviation pioneer—became the first of a long line of U.S. Navy aircraft carriers.

Another boost for aviation—although at times of questionable value, and definitely so overstated that its true value was to be obscured in a flood of emotion—was to come from the efforts of Brigadier General William L. Mitchell, an Army officer who had organized and commanded the Army Air Forces in Europe during the war, to promote a combined single-service air arm.

Ever since the introduction of the military airplane, there had been occasional congressional proposals directed at establishing such a single-service air force, but these had not met with much success. Under the impetus of the favorable publicity received by the air forces in the war—much of which was sensationalized and greatly exaggerated—another attempt along these lines was launched in the spring of 1919 with the establishment of the American Aviation Mission, headed by the Assistant Secretary of War. It was directed to make a complete study of the aviation industry at home and abroad, and to subsequently formulate proposals that would promote civil aviation, and at the same time ensure compatibility with military requirements in case of national emergency. This mission

[196]

recommended formation of a Department of Aeronautics, with Cabinet rank.

The Secretary of War, however, was not convinced that this was the answer, and moved in June 1919 to form a Joint Army-Navy Board of Aeronautics. This board defined the bounds of Army and Navy aviation; laid the groundwork for future cooperation between the services; and made provisions for a mutual sharing of technological advances. And on that logical and amicable foundation, the matter might well have rested, but for the emphatic intervention of General "Billy" Mitchell.

It was his contention that not only should aviation be made a separate service, but that the Army and the Navy had both been rendered obsolete by the invention of the military airplane, and he was not shy in making his views known to the public at large. Mitchell was a public relations genius without parallel in American military history, and his method was simple: to get the public on his side through a steady stream of newspaper and magazine articles, and then, with the firm backing of public opinion, to convince the military and political leaders of the rectitude of his position.

Tangible evidence to support his views was, however, somewhat lacking, and even General Pershing cautioned against overeager expansion of the air arm. "Enthusiasts often forget the obligations of military aviation to other troops," he commented, "and sometimes credit that service with ability to achieve results in war that have not received practical demonstration." But an opportunity for Mitchell to point with triumph at what could only be regarded, in the public eye, as a "practical demonstration" was to come with a series of Navy-conducted tests beginning in November 1920.

These tests were held in order to obtain data on the effectiveness of different size bombs, information about the ability of an airplane to locate a ship at sea, and comparisons of the structural strength and watertight integrity of various hull designs when subjected to aerial attack. It was not so much the intention to sink the targets as it was to inspect and measure the damage at each stage of the tests.

The old battleship *Indiana*, a veteran of the Spanish-American

War, was the first target. In the first phase, some dummy bombs were dropped from airplanes, both for practice and to get some indication of the percentage of hits that could be expected under control conditions, with the ship dead in the water. For the next phase, several large bombs were positioned on or near the ship and detonated by remote control. One of these resulted in the flooding and sinking of *Indiana*. No live bombs had been dropped from any airplane in this test.

But Mitchell—who had not been near the tests—took this result as proof of his contention that the Navy was obsolete: surface ships could quickly and completely be put out of action by airplanes. He went before Congress and made the interesting statement that "We can tell you definitely now that we can either destroy or sink any ship in existence today . . . give us the warships to attack and come and watch it."

The Navy was shocked that the Congress was taking testimony on such an important subject from an officer without any experience in naval matters, and sent a complaint to Congress. This pointed out that the Navy had been conducting bombing exercises against moving targets for several years, compiling data on this aspect of operations which was of natural concern and interest to the Navy, and deplored the fact that the Navy had not been invited to present its views. But, then, Mitchell had not been "invited" either, in the formal sense. The son of a U.S. senator, he had a few useful contacts in the Congress and never hesitated to use them.

Another series of tests were to be held in the spring of 1921, using other old American ships and some German ships which had been turned over to the United States for destruction as part of the international peace agreements. Secretary of the Navy Edwin Denby invited the Army to participate in these new tests, which were to be held about 90 miles out to sea, to lessen the danger to surface shipping (gunfire as well as bombing was to be involved), and because the water was sufficiently deep that the ships, when the tests had been completed, would pose no navigational hazard and could not be salvaged by any nation looking for a ready-made navy. The first of the tests was to be a search effort and dummy bombing attack on a radio-controlled ship underway at sea, moving at about 10 knots. Mitchell was impatient; he was not interested in any dummy bombing, nor was he interested in having to search for a ship. He accused the Navy—in the public press—of holding the tests too far out at sea; that this posed unnecessary hazard for the pilots of land-based airplanes; and that the Navy was deliberately trying to reduce the chances of any of the targets being sunk.

It was universally acknowledged within the Navy that an airplane could easily sink a ship, if it dropped enough high-explosives on or near it. But the problem would be, in wartime, for an airplane to penetrate the antiaircraft defenses of the ship, and to then be able to drop its bombs with sufficient accuracy on a maneuvering target in order to hit it. (In British tests conducted in 1924, with a radically maneuvering radio-controlled ship, 114 bombs were dropped from altitudes of from 5,000 to 12,000 feet—and not one single hit was recorded.) But such realistic considerations were of little concern to General Mitchell. His program now was pegged to the slogan "Planes can sink ships," and his immediate goal was to prove it.

Accordingly, he requested that some ships be turned over to the Army for his own use; and this request was granted. He was given five ships, including three battleships, and a series of tests began— some independently by the Army and the Navy, some with cooperation between the Army and the Navy, and some in concert but without much cooperation. The target ships were sunk, some of them quite easily. But this had been expected: most of the ships had only the most rudimentary watertight compartmentation; all were dead in the water; the weather was ideal; the attacks were made at low altitudes; and there were no personnel aboard any of them to exercise basic damage-control techniques, such as patching leaks and pumping out water.

The most famous of the tests was the sinking of the German battleship *Ostfriesland*, which was about 50 per cent larger and a few years newer than the American target ships, but was not of a particularly advanced design. The sinking of the *Ostfriesland* is preserved forever in dramatic motion pictures taken at the scene, which seem to show the once proud ship being rapidly destroyed by the invincible airplane. In point of fact, the test with this ship lasted over a period of two days, with 69 planes dropping a total of 69 bombs—with only 16 hits—from altitudes of 1,200 to 2,000 feet. The ship was damaged and weakened with each attack, and progressive flooding—which had started in small degree even before the tests began—seriously reduced its potential for survival. The last attack, in which six 2,000-pound bombs were dropped with no hits but three near-misses close enough to do extensive injury to the hull, finished the *Ostfriesland*. She sank within ten minutes. But this was almost 24 hours after the first attacks had been made.

The tests were to continue for several years, and the results proved many things—including the relative invulnerability of a well-designed hull, with heavy armored decks, to attacks by the airplanes of that period—but Mitchell did not let the facts of the case interfere with public appreciation of the results. He had made his point, and the Navy could thereafter only try to keep the matter in proper perspective—without much success.

But it must be acknowledged that there was some positive benefit from the controversy and the tests: they focused attention, public and congressional, upon the airplane. And the exuberant young aviators, Army and Navy alike, masters of a new and wondrous element, could only thrive on publicity.

As for the rest of the Navy—well, the problems of the aviation branch were of but minimal concern; aviation was, after all, only a small and relatively experimental part of a large and dynamic organization. The bombing tests were primarily conducted to obtain information to help improve the basic weapons of that organization, and General Mitchell's campaign to promote a consolidated air service (which did not achieve its main objective) was of only passing interest to the majority of naval leaders. As it turned out, they were suddenly to be faced with a crisis of compelling magnitude: the prospect of losing most of the magnificent fleet which they had been so long in building up.

When the war had ended; when the cheering of the crowds had ceased and citizen-sailors had returned to their homes, the Navy returned to its own prewar activities. The 1916 building program, which had been in large part suspended because of the shift in emphasis to the smaller ships, came under discussion; and in 1919, after careful consideration, the General Board and the Secretary of the Navy decided to pick up where they had left off in 1917—one battleship keel had been laid before work was halted. This could have been an ideal opportunity to update the plans of the 16 capital ships, and to incorporate the benefits of new developments and advanced technology. Although there were no pressures of any kind for the early addition of new ships to the fleet, it was quickly decided that there was no reason to modify any of the original plans, except those of the battle cruisers—a class which had proven inadequate at the Battle of Jutland. Of the fourteen British and German battle cruisers engaged, four had been sunk and seven badly damaged almost in a matter of minutes; this tended to indicate that increased armor protection might be useful, and American designs were altered accordingly.

Even without any improvements, the ships of the 1916 program were indeed formidable: the smallest of the ten battleships was to be 624 feet in length, displace 32,600 tons, and carry eight 16-inch guns at a speed of 21 knots. The six battle cruisers were to be 874 feet in length, displace 35,300 tons, and also carry eight 16-inch guns, but at a speed of 35 knots. The Navy already had in commission at this time sixteen first-class battleships, none of which were built before 1910, and fifteen pre-dreadnought battleships. And here, a curious fact must be considered: there was no longer a German navy to threaten the security of the United States. This very threat had been the main impetus for the 1916 program; and, in fact, the only other navy in the world of any consequence was the British, which

[201]

was overloaded with obsolete ships and, as a more or less permanent ally, posed no threat at all. But the Navy Department had its authorizations already and, without any regard to the realities of the world situation, proceeded to cash them in. The keels for all sixteen big ships were dutifully laid down.

However, the prospect of watching the U.S. Navy acquire, hands down, the most powerful fleet in the world was not a pleasant one for the British, who might have felt constrained, no matter what the cost, to enter into a competitive building race that would have benefited neither country. There was also another foreign power that could view the same prospect with some misgivings; the Japanese, who, having risen to a place of ascendancy in Asiatic waters, could not help but regard such a move as a direct threat to their own interests.

And at home in the United States there were many people who found it difficult to see any rationale in the Navy program. The war was over; the world was at peace; and the instruments of peace—treaties, agreements, and the goodwill of all nations—were now to be favored over the machines of war. While Congress failed to approve United States participation in the League of Nations, that did not prevent the nations of the world from working together to maintain the peace by curtailing armaments. Under pressure from all sides at home and abroad to promote the twin causes of peace and economy, President Warren G. Harding, who succeeded Wilson in 1921, dusted off a strange clause that had been built into the 1916 authorizations. The provisions of that act had declared it to be the "policy of the United States to adjust and settle its international disputes through mediation and arbitration" rather than war, and authorized the President to at any time invite a conference of all the great governments to formulate a plan of arbitration and "consider the question of disarmament." The act stipulated that if international reduction of armament could be secured, any of the ships authorized therein but not at that time under contract were not to be built.

Wilson himself had acknowledged that a naval appropriation act

[202]

was "a most unusual place" for such a statement of policy; but at the time the act was being deliberated the cause of peace and neutrality was ascendant, and it is most probable that this particular clause merely was included to help smooth the passage of the unprecedented shipbuilding program. Be that as it may, it now became the basis for an international conference, held at Washington, on the general subject of naval disarmament.

The Washington Conference was convened on November 12, 1921, and was to last for twelve weeks. It was sponsored not by the Navy Department but by the State Department, and the Navy was not soon to forgive that branch of the government for what was to come. Essentially, and at the express suggestion of Secretary of State Charles Evans Hughes, all naval building programs in the major navies of the world were to be conducted on a set quota: the United States and Great Britain were to have parity with an allowed 500,000 tons of capital ships each; Japan was permitted 300,000 tons; and France and Italy, 175,000 tons apiece. Aircraft-carrier tonnage was set at the same 5:5:3:1.75 ratio, with the United States and Great Britain allowed 135,000 tons each, with no single carrier to be over 27,000 tons' displacement. (A clause was included to allow the United States to convert two of the battle-cruiser hulls into the *Lexington* and *Saratoga*, weighing 33,000 tons each; the other nations enjoyed similar special privileges as long as overall tonnage quotas were not exceeded.) A few of the major ships then under construction in each of the countries might be completed; all others were to be scrapped, along with numbers of older obsolete battleships and some miscellaneous types, and a ten-year abstinence in the construction of battleships was to be observed. Another important clause provided that a *status quo* was to be maintained in regard to fortification of certain areas in the Pacific.

The treaty was ratified, but not without opposition from the Navy, which stoutly maintained that multilateral agreements were no substitute for naval supremacy when it came to national security. But as it turned out, most of the agreements were to be kept by all signatories for thirteen years; and the conditions of the treaty were, in the long run, to stand to the benefit of the Navy. The old and useless battleships headed for the scrap heap. Construction of all but three of the magnificent new battleships (which were, considering the international situation, just as useless) was canceled, along with the four remaining battle cruisers. The money and effort that would have been put into building these unnecessary ships and in maintaining the other ships, were redirected into fresh new fields: into the development and perfection of those weapons which had but recently made their mark—the airplane, the aircraft carrier, the submarine, the destroyer.

The Navy did not realize it yet, but another era had come to an end.

It had been an era conceived in the writings of Mahan, given birth at the hands of a small group of militaristic politicians, and baptized in the virtually bloodless war with Spain; it was an era that saw the United States enter the world arena with all the pluck and confidence of a brash young newcomer, to emerge as a power with which to be reckoned. It was an era symbolized by the battleship, the queen of the seas that went through her brief life cycle without achieving the promised fulfillment—battle with an enemy fleet of her peers.

That fleet had never come calling, and who can say but what, had the queen not been at home, the fleet would have come uninvited? Wars of the nineteenth century, as someone has observed, most frequently did occur between a strong, poor nation and a weak, rich one; and the United States of 1890 was so weak that Rudyard Kipling characterized it "as unprotected as a jellyfish," and so rich that he added "there is ransom and loot past the counting of man on her seaboard alone—a plunder that would enrich a nation."

The United States of 1900 was no longer unprotected: the queen of the seas had put a stinger in the tail of the jellyfish. The United States of 1910 had the second largest collection of battleships in the world, and in 1920 was approaching naval superiority.

But the Age of the Battleship was over. The queen of the seas had found a place in the sun, but the day had been short. With very few exceptions, after the Battle of Jutland, never again were the ships of any battle fleet to come together in massive confrontation; and, while the battleship was to be further developed in succeeding years, it was to find its future place in the naval arsenal in support of amphibious landings, in shore bombardment, and antiaircraft defense. And it was eventually to disappear from the navies of the world, to be enshrined in memory and in landlocked memorials where some of the few surviving examples of the type were to be placed on public display.

The U.S. Navy had come a long way from the doldrums of 1881. It had risen in strength and efficiency to be placed on a par with the largest navy in the world. It had risen in spite of internal bungling and congressional bumbling; in spite of cyclic indifference and parochial blindness.

It would continue to rise, through several periods of war and peace, to a position where, under a completely different set of international circumstances, it would be virtually larger and stronger than all of the other navies in the world put together.

Index